Debates in Psychology

Debates in Psychology tackles some of the major issues and controversies within the field of psychology. The book includes a discussion of the major debates in psychology prescribed by the AQA (A) level syllabus, such as free will and determinism, whether or not psychology can (or indeed should) be a science, reductionism, and the nature–nurture debate. Additionally, the 'mind–body question' is examined as an example of reductionism in psychology. A chapter on behaviourism is also included in order to draw together the debates covered throughout the book.

Each topic covered in *Debates in Psychology* is presented in a highly readable and accessible manner. The book will be invaluable for students wishing to gain a greater understanding of this exciting area.

Andy Bell is Senior Lecturer in Psychology at the Manchester Metropolitan University.

Routledge Modular Psychology

Series editors: Cara Flanagan is a Reviser for AS and A2 level Psychology and lectures at Inverness College. Philip Banyard is Associate Senior Lecturer in Psychology at Nottingham Trent University and a Chief Examiner for AS and A2 level Psychology. Both are experienced writers.

The *Routledge Modular Psychology* series is a completely new approach to introductory-level psychology, tailor-made to the new modular style of teaching. Each short book covers a topic in more detail than any large textbook can, allowing teacher and student to select material exactly to suit any particular course or project.

The books have been written especially for those students new to higher-level study, whether at school, college or university. They include specially designed features to help with technique, such as a model essay at an average level with an examiner's comments to show how extra marks can be gained.

The *Routledge Modular Psychology* texts are all user-friendly and accessible and include the following features:

- practice essays with specialist commentary to show how to achieve a higher grade
- chapter summaries to assist with revision
- progress and review exercises
- glossary of key terms
- summaries of key research
- further reading to stimulate ongoing study and research
- cross-referencing to other books in the series

Also available in this series (titles listed by syllabus section):

Debates in Psychology

Andy Bell

First published 2002 by Routledge
27 Church Road, Hove, East Sussex, BN3 2FA

Simultaneously published in the USA and Canada
by Taylor & Francis, Inc
29 West 35th Street, New York, NY 10001

Routledge is an imprint of the Taylor & Francis Group

© 2002 Andy Bell

Typeset in Times and Frutiger by Keystroke,
Jacaranda Lodge, Wolverhampton
Printed and bound in Great Britain
by TJ International Ltd, Padstow, Cornwall

Cover design by Terry Foley

British Library Cataloguing in Publication Data
A catalogue record for this book is available from the British Library

ISBN 0–415–19268–4 (hbk)
ISBN 0–415–19269–2 (pbk)

In memory of Mark Horton
(1963–1997)

For my daughters, Amy & Georgia

Contents

Illustrations

Acknowledgement

AQA (AEB) examination questions are reproduced by permission of the Assessment and Qualifications Alliance.

Introduction to debates in psychology

- Psychology and philosophy
- How this text is structured
- Knowledge and truth in psychology
- How the debates relate to each other
- Summary

Psychology and philosophy

The 'debates' covered in this text concern philosophical issues related to psychology. The word *philosophy* comes from Greek and literally means 'love of wisdom/truth'. Thus, this text is mainly concerned with presenting a series of debates which examine just how 'true' various beliefs are concerning psychology. For example, Chapter Four includes arguments for and against the idea or belief that mind and body are separate, but somehow causally connected, 'things'. But just how reasonable is it to hold such a belief? Any individual may hold many beliefs, but clearly not all beliefs are necessarily true.

When a debate is held in Parliament, individual politicians provide arguments for and against certain stances (or positions) concerning a particular issue. The strength of an argument should ideally be related to just how convincing a particular argument is. In other words, it should be related to how 'true' the line of argument being proposed is considered to be. This is inevitably related to an appraisal of the evidence presented by the speaker to support what is being said. The same applies to the various debates in psychology covered here. Each chapter presents arguments and evidence for and against the particular issues addressed. Just as politicians debating in Parliament may hold very different and often completely opposing views, the same can be said of psychologists. The reader of this text, then, should try to be engaged in weighing up the evidence presented. Indeed, good answers to questions posed in the A-level psychology examination will do just that. They will present a balanced and logical argument which fully addresses different positions held by different psychologists on a particular issue.

How this text is structured

It is intended that each chapter here builds upon material already presented. Thus when Chapter Five is reached concerning whether or not psychology can be a science, key debates covered in the chapters that precede this are brought back into the discussion. If free will (Chapter Two) is an illusion and all behaviour and mental life is the result of deterministic chains of cause-and-effect relationships, then establishing these relationships very much fits in with the traditional goal of the scientific endeavour. And thus, logically psychology should adopt a 'scientific' approach. The issue of reductionism is dealt with in Chapter Three and here the emphasis is upon whether or not it is fruitful for psychologists to break down human beings into smaller units in order to understand how they work. This approach again is quite typical of what is often meant when we refer to science. This is followed by an account (Chapter Four) of the mind–body problem. Here, it is intended as a good illustration of the problems inherent in scientific reductionism.

After Chapter Five has attempted to tie together issues raised in the preceding chapters, there follows an account (Chapter Six) of the nature–nurture debate. This prepares the ground for the chapter which follows on behaviourism. Here the validity and usefulness of behaviourism's extreme environmentalist argument – nurture – are examined.

Knowledge and truth in psychology

The debate as to whether or not psychology should or could be a science (Chapter Five) is really concerned with issues related to how knowledge is collected and interpreted by psychologists. It also concerns the truth status of knowledge. In other words, the extent to which such knowledge is actually true. Some methods (or approaches) to psychology are, of course, more scientific than others. What this really often means is that some approaches to gaining knowledge in psychology are more objective than others. However, many psychologists would argue that the main problem associated with objectivity is that the inner world of the individual lies outside of the publicly observable, objectively available, domain. Now, the problem with this is that surely this inner world is exactly what psychologists should really be interested in.

This concern for subjectivity and objectivity has given rise in recent years to the so-called *qualitative–quantitative* issue in psychology. Whereas some psychologists would insist that the only true way of gaining knowledge is by direct measurement of readily observable facts, others insist that other methods are more appropriate. Objective measurement of reaction times and information processing speeds may well be an effective way of conducting research in cognitive psychology. But when, for example, it comes to investigating the psychological and emotional impact that divorce has on married couples, would it not be more productive to *ask* men and women actually involved in the process of divorce about their own subjective experiences? In other words, would it not be more fruitful to put to one side the obsession with objectivity that is associated with traditional science, and in its place to make subjective experiences the focus of study? In this example, this would involve taking the things that men and women might say about their own personal and private thoughts and feelings, etc., as representing the 'truth'. If philosophy is defined as 'love of wisdom/truth', then doesn't it make sense to argue that what the individuals themselves have to say somehow gets closer to the truth in terms of how events have impacted upon them?

The final topic of debate to be addressed in this text (Chapter Seven) concerns *behaviourism*. As will clearly be understood, *behaviourism* is not just an approach to psychology – it is a philosophical position. And this can be described as a philosophical position because the behaviouristic approach, as will be seen, insisted that only publicly observable behaviour was to be taken as 'true' data. Again, we come back to this idea of 'love of wisdom/truth'. Now, behaviourism's approach, as will be seen, insisted upon establishing truth from the researcher's point of view. What the animal (usually a rat or a pigeon) actually did was objectively observed and measured by the investigator. By adopting this approach, behaviourism claimed somehow to get close to an undeniable truth concerning exactly what caused an animal to behave in a particular manner. On the other hand, the move towards the qualitative approach described in the example concerning divorce is also a move towards a 'love of wisdom/truth'. But in this case it is not a question of truth from the point of view of the researcher. On the contrary, the viewpoint of those who are actually the subjects of the research is here made of central importance. Here the emphasis shifts away from the 'truth' as the researcher sees it, to the 'truth' as those actually under observation might see it.

How the debates relate to each other

The various debates covered in this text tend inevitably to overlap and to cross-relate to each other. For example, one position on the mind–body question (Chapter Four) is referred to as 'materialism'. This proposes that what we call the mind can actually be reduced to physical processes. Chapter Four provides arguments for and against reduction-ism with reference to the mind–body problem. As such this provides a detailed example of the issue of reductionism that precedes this in Chapter Three. This also relates to Chapter Five because if mind really is reducible to physical brain processes, then this implies that psychology itself should ultimately concentrate on solving the mystery of the mind at the levels of biology and physics. And biology and physics have had great success as traditional sciences. If human beings are really reducible to a complex collection of atoms, then those atoms all obey the laws of physics just like anything else in the world, and thus, logically, it can be asserted that they can be studied in the same way as the natural sciences.

Behaviourism is covered in the final chapter because it is intended to provide a good illustration of the issues already presented in the chapters that precede this. It should hopefully become very clear just why this particular debate is so connected to the other issues dealt with throughout this book. A student answering a question in an examination concerning any of the debates in psychology covered in the syllabus should find that much of the material provided in the chapter on *behaviourism* can be drawn upon in order to illustrate the answer to that particular question. For example, in terms of the nature–nurture debate (Chapter Six), behaviourism comes down strongly on the side of environmental determinism (nurture). Behaviourism of course is thus a position which argues very convincingly against the idea of free will (Chapter Two).

Chapter Two, Free will and determinism, examines the extent to which our behaviour, and indeed the way that we think, is the product of free choice. The common sense view tends to be that it's just a fact that people tend to regard themselves as being free and that, as we go through our daily lives, we actually feel that we make decisions and choices that come from within. Furthermore, these choices are then responsible for directing our behaviour. Extreme behaviourists however, such as Skinner and Watson, proposed that all behaviour is the product of environmental factors. Far from being a product from within, behaviour is seen as being shaped by events in the world outside.

Summary

Each chapter presented here is designed to stand alone in presenting arguments for and against various positions concerning the debates that are covered. This text, however, should be read in full. As has been outlined above, the debates *themselves* do not really stand in isolation. They relate to each other. In answering an examination question concerning a particular debate, a good essay, whilst actually answering the question set, will point out the ways in which other debates can, and must, be referred to. Material from various chapters can be presented in order to illustrate various points. Thus an essay on the nature–nurture debate may well need to cite behaviourism as a strong environmental (nurture) stance. The materialist position on the mind–body question is essentially an argument for one type of reductionism. An essay on free will may include comments concerning the ways in which both nature and nurture dictate and shape human behaviour and experience. And so on. As you read through this book, make notes concerning some of the connections that are made, and perhaps some that you think of yourself, between the various debates. Doing this would be helpful to you with respect to the final *Review exercise* in Chapter Seven.

Further reading

Hospers, J. (1990) *An Introduction to Philosophical Analysis*, 3rd edn, London: Routledge.
Hospers' text provides further reading on (1) the mind–body debate; (2) free will and (3) scientific knowledge. It also serves as a good reference text for philosophy generally. Hospers illustrates his arguments with many clear and useful everyday examples. This makes the text very readable. Although perhaps a little more advanced than A-level.

Free will and determinism

What exactly is the free will and determinism debate?
Why the problem concerning free will persists
Science and causal relationships
Psychology and causal relationships
Determinism and fatalism
The construct of free will
Psychology, science and free will
Is our behaviour determined and predictable?
Ethological studies
Free will and responsibility
Feeling free and being free
Existentialism
Summary

What exactly is the free will and determinism debate?

This debate concerns the extent to which it is reasonable to assume that our behaviour is under our own control. Those who believe that this is so would argue that individuals possess some kind of internal *agent* that directs behaviour. The term agent simply means anything that produces an effect. Manufacturers of soap powders often refer to their product as a 'cleaning agent'. This means that their product has the desired effect of cleaning clothes. To believe that human beings possess free will, then, is to believe that human beings possess something inside themselves which can produce an effect on their own behaviour. This something is often referred to as free will. It is important to stress that this thing called free will must act independently of all external forces. The other side of the argument is presented by those who believe in determinism. This term means that our behaviour is caused by forces beyond our own control.

The issue concerning free will and determinism is particularly difficult to address for a variety of important reasons. Indeed, students doing a degree in psychology at university are usually faced at some point in their studies with examination questions such as: Is belief in free will rational?; Is all of our behaviour determined?; Do we determine our own thoughts and beliefs?; To what extent are we free? And so on.

For a number of reasons, the very fact that the question continues to be posed at all is probably quite a healthy state of affairs. One of the main reasons being that, unlike in physics where it is generally agreed that the world follows more or less lawful, and hence determined and determinable, paths, the world that psychologists study is not quite so straightforward. At least to some extent, human beings are often considered to be self-determining in a way that, for example, a tree or a volcano is not.

Why the problem concerning free will persists

The free will and determinism debate inevitably involves the issue of causation. Put simply, if it is true that every event in the world is caused by something else, then this would not only include the physical world out there, it must also include ourselves because we too are a part of the world. In other words, it would suggest that human behaviour and experience, the subject matter of psychology, are also determined by causal chains. And if we are really the product of causal chains, then how could we ever be said to be free? This question is now addressed in some detail.

Science and causal relationships

Another popular question that students will often face concerns the appraisal of whether or not the discipline of psychology is, or indeed ever could be, a science. Most people's understanding of scientific endeavour is that science should concern itself with knowing the world. In particular, this concerns knowing about causal relationships within the world. Terms related to the word science, or usually related to – or applied to – the activity of scientists, concern their attempts at objectivity in establishing what the causal relationships might be. Hence, the scientist needs to observe the world in order to see exactly what influences or causes what, under what circumstances, etc. What are the determining factors associated with one thing happening rather than another?

Establishing causation

The emphasis here, then, is upon objective observation rather than subjective speculation about how the world actually works. In order to establish what it is that actually influences or causes what, the scientist conducts observable experiments. These, of course, often involve the manipulation of a possible causal factor, termed the independent variable, in order to observe what effect such manipulation might have upon another, *dependent*, variable. This way of establishing causal relationships, of course, has been prevalent in psychology. The following example is presented as an illustration.

Milgram (1963) conducted an experiment where participants were required to administer electric shocks with increasing severity to confederates of the experimenter. Each time the confederate made an error in a memory test, a shock was to be given as 'punishment'. Of course, no shocks were really administered at all. The real issue under investigation by Milgram had nothing to do with memory; it concerned just how far participants would go in administering the shocks. The study thus involved deception and was in fact concerned with examining the extent to which participants would obey the experimenter's instruction to shock the confederate. When the experiment had been completed, many participants stated that the reason for or cause of their behaviour was that they were deferring to the authority of Yale University. That is, that although they were anxious about their own behaviour, i.e. 'administering' harmful electric shocks, they frequently reported after the experiment was completed that they didn't really believe that a prestigious university such as Yale would allow an experiment to proceed that would do any lasting harm. Here, then, participants were reporting on one of the causes of their willingness to continue administering the electric shocks. This causal factor was identified as participants somehow feeling safe in having the famous institution of Yale University behind them. Thus, following what J. S. Mill termed the 'rule of one variable', Milgram repeated his experiments in a city centre location without mentioning to the participants that the experiments had anything to do with Yale. Of course, the 'rule of one variable' here means that in order to see to what extent obedience is due to the location in which the experiment was conducted, it is necessary that the experimenter should vary only one aspect of the experimental set-up. In this case, the location. All other aspects of the experiment should be repeated in exactly the same manner.

Milgram observed that obedience remained high, although some drop in the level of intensity of shocks administered was noted. In this way, then, the experiment allows the scientist/psychologist the framework within which to tease out causal relationships, not only what might be causing what to happen, but, importantly, to what extent or degree a cause–effect relationship can be observed. In this example, then, it can be said that the location in which the experiment took place was the *independent variable*. Hence it was discovered that people are more obedient in certain situations/locations. The *dependent variable* here being the level of obedience measured by the experimenter.

Progress exercise

Read thoroughly, and carefully examine *Research article* **3** in Chapter Eight. Write down which is (a) the *independent variable* and (b) the *dependent variable*.

Thus it seems quite clear that scientists, and those psychologists wishing to be 'scientific', have made great progress by identifying causal relationships. Indeed the 'pure' sciences have achieved enormous technological advances by adhering to a view of the macro universe that is causal, mechanistic and, hence, determined. Scientists are interested in establishing that the world behaves in a lawful manner.

And it is only by discovering what the lawful regularities of the world actually are that the scientist is able to make predictions and control the natural world. The difficult question, then, concerning whether or not humans have free will really involves an examination of whether or not it is a legitimate or logical step to import the mechanistic successes of the natural sciences to the discipline of psychology.

Psychology and causal relationships

People generally have little difficulty in considering as a fact the idea that the natural world obeys mechanistic laws. Nor do they have difficulty in accepting that such laws have great predictive power. For example, such laws of nature include the 'hard' fact that water will always boil at 212° F at sea level. Another law is the fact that the **refractive index** of light as it passes between one medium and another – say, from air to glass or from air to water – is always a predictable constant and hence can be calculated in advance. (The word 'predict', of course, simply meaning to be able to 'say before' we actually observe the world what will in fact happen in it.) But how do people tend to feel when the suggestion is made that because human beings are an integral part of the natural world, then it can also quite logically be said that they too are determined? Most people actually find it quite offensive to suggest that there is nothing special about being human. Many would claim that it is quite contrary to our experience of ourselves to propose that we are just as determined as any other part of the world. Somehow, it is emotionally upsetting to believe that although the factors that determine us might be more complex than those which determine a fruitfly, the ocean, an ant or a stone . . . we are, nonetheless, a part of the world, and hence just as determined as any other part of it.

The difference between 'free will' and 'hope'

Some would claim that this problem is largely to do with the different manner in which we tend to deal with and experience ourselves and the way in which we confront the rest of the world. For example, as you read this text, it might be raining heavily outside. Your attitude to the rain would tend to be one of resignation to the way things are. Hence, you might think or hope that it might soon blow over. That is, you might hope that something else will *cause* the rain to cease. For example, you might hope that the strength and direction of the wind might send the clouds, and hence the rain, elsewhere. So much for the way in which you might experience the outside world. However, as you continue reading, it would be rather odd for you to think: 'Oh, I do hope that I shall continue to read this chapter. I have an essay to write concerning free will and reading this might just give me some good ideas.' Surely it is much more likely that you will find yourself thinking that, as an effort of will, you are going to continue reading the text and grapple with the ideas proposed within it. You do not *hope* that this will be the case in the same way that you hope that the rain will cease. Giving up or continuing with the task is a matter of your strength of will. It's not a matter of hope at all. It's up to you, so to speak. So, talking and thinking about what the rain might do is very different from how we talk and think about what we personally should, or could, do. An individual can be said to have a personal responsibility towards their own study of psychology but cannot be said to be held responsible for the rain. Nor is the rain in any way considered somehow magically able to stop itself. So the way in which we look at human nature is readily seen as quite different to the way in which we look at the rest of nature.

Free will and responsibility

The above illustration touches upon the inevitable link between responsibility and free will. Although we cannot act upon the rain, free will proposes logically that we can act upon ourselves; that we are not slaves to deterministic forces. It could be argued that because we possess free will, we have the capacity and the moral obligation to do what we ought to do, rather than what external forces command. Free will proposes an inner imperative or command. This idea, of course, is quite at odds with the determinism proposed by, for example, behaviourism (Chapter Seven). We return to the issue of responsibility and its relationship with free will later in this chapter.

Is free will an illusion?

Dealing effectively with the world largely concerns making predictions based upon notions of determinism: looking for regularities, orderliness, patterns, etc. Indeed if we didn't approach the world in this manner, we would have great difficulty in functioning at all. However, for some reason, when it comes to ourselves, we seem to put determinism to one side and in its place *invent* the idea that free will really exists. Now this notion of free will effectively means that if you have just behaved in one way, you could easily have chosen to behave in another manner, even if all the circumstances had been the same. You did one thing, but you could just as easily have done something else. You raised your right arm but could have raised your left without anything changing at all in terms of both external circumstances and the inner, biological, events going on inside of your brain, when you decide which arm to raise.

The important question, of course, concerns whether or not what we call 'free will' is anything more than a construct of our own making. Whether or not this thing that we call free will really exists is quite another matter. Consider carefully the following statement:

We experience ourselves as having the freedom to act in a different manner to the way in which we in fact have chosen to act. When we do something we are able to say that we did it because we have free will, and, importantly, we did it and could have done otherwise if we had willed to do otherwise. Furthermore, we could have willed to do so without anything at all changing in terms of inner or outer environmental circumstances.

There are several important points for consideration that the last paragraph provokes. These are addressed in the next sections.

Determinism and fatalism

It should be noticeable that in writing the last sentence of the paragraph in question, great care was taken to avoid terms such as 'deliberating' or 'deciding'. Exercising free will is quite different to what we mean when we talk about 'coming to a decision' or weighing up the pros and cons of particular courses of action that are available. A determinist would, of course, claim that, unlike free will, these kinds of mental deliberations have determined outcomes. That is, that the person deliberating will inevitably make a decision which is based upon an evaluation of the positive and negative effects of similar past behaviour or courses of action. The person's own personal history will determine the outcome. Or their own particular way of thinking about the alternatives will in some way contribute to the eventual decision taken. Ways of thinking are, of course, similarly the result of experience. An individual, for example, who finally chooses a particularly risky course of action after deliberation may, in the past, have found risky behaviour rewarding. That such behaviour 'paid off'. That, overall, the resulting benefits outweighed the costs, and so on. Thus, the determinist would claim that just because the outcome of deliberation is actually determined, this doesn't imply that individuals will ever be free from having to go through the anguish of deliberation itself. Fatalism on the other hand implies an attitude that if everything is already determined, then why bother deliberating? Just do anything without going through the mental ordeal of deciding. Determinism, however, does not imply the same stance as fatalism. Perhaps it is just our lot as human beings that we are condemned to those very aspects of life which indeed make us human: the anguish of deliberation and the responsibility that surrounds our decisions. Perhaps it is this very anguish that makes us free or, at least, which gives us the illusion that we are free.

What is wrong with making untestable statements?

What does it actually mean to claim that free will implies that we '*could have done otherwise if we had willed to do otherwise. And could have willed to do so without anything at all changing in terms of inner or outer environmental circumstances*'?

If you think about this statement for a little while, it should become clear that it doesn't really offer much evidence for free will at all. Imagine that you are in a café and the waiter asks you what you would like to drink. At that very point in time, you will be immersed in a variety of inner circumstances. For example, you feel very thirsty, but you don't really want to drink anything that contains alcohol, because you have a meeting to attend with your boss at work and even a small amount of alcohol tends to make you feel drowsy, and you need to be alert when dealing with her. On the other hand, you feel nervous about the meeting. Perhaps it will make you feel a little more relaxed. But then again, you don't really want your boss to smell alcohol on your breath just after midday. These, then, are the sort of inner 'realities' which you consider as the waiter hangs around waiting for your answer. (Perhaps that's why they are called 'waiters'!) What about the *outer* environmental circumstances? These may include the fact that the few clouds that were there have just blown over, and it really does look as though it's going to continue to be a hot day. Perhaps you should have a beer after all to cool you down. Several more customers have just poured into the café. The waiter seems to be getting a little impatient, as there are now more people to serve. You come to a decision and order a glass of lemonade.

Now this seems to be a fairly reasonable decision to make given the circumstances. But is it really reasonable to say that at the very moment when you ordered the lemonade, you could have done something different without any of the inner or outer circumstances changing? This proposal is really what free will seems to imply. That you could have willed yourself to order an iced coffee or a cup of tea. Both of these alternatives seem to be quite reasonable too. So why is there any problem in suggesting that you could have done other than what you actually decided to do? Don't we often feel that we could just have easily chosen Y rather than X in any situation similar to that described above? Isn't that just the way it feels when we make a decision? We did one thing, but could just as easily have done another.

Well, the two main objections to this would be as follows. Firstly, the proposal is untestable. It would be impossible to replicate all of the inner and outer circumstances just to test the claim that another decision actually was possible. So the proposal itself has no real power to convince us that free will really exists.

The difference between feeling *free and actually* being *free*

Secondly, there is a problem with the claim that, as we go through life, we actually *feel* free. At every moment we feel that alternatives are open to us to do *other* than what we actually do. But finally, we do live our life one way, rather than another. We make decisions XYZ, rather than ABC. There's no point saying that you moved to London when you could just as easily have stayed in Paris. You didn't stay in Paris. And that's the end of it. Let us assume that Paris was not cut off by The Plague and that entry and exit from this city were allowed at the time that you came back to London. On that level, it cannot be denied that you were, so to speak, politically free to make a choice between staying in Paris or leaving. Perhaps it's more reasonable to assume that there were a variety of factors that you weighed up in making your decision to leave. You missed your friends. You were struggling with the language. Or perhaps there were personal psychological factors of which you were not even consciously aware. Determinism would claim that you were no more free to stay in Paris than you were to order the beer rather than the lemonade. There exists a whole array of internal and external determining factors surrounding any decision. As will be outlined later, such determining factors are not necessarily conscious. Psychoanalytic theory indeed suggests that much of our behaviour is determined due to inner forces over which we have little or no control. Feeling free and actually being free are two very different things.

A counter-argument to the above statement, however, is that when we come to talking about happiness, would we really say to someone: 'It's all very well you telling me that you really feel happy at this point in your life, but what do you know? Feeling happy and being happy are very different things.' This would probably get the reply: 'Well, if I feel happy, then that's good enough for me. I'd rather not know whether or not I really am, if you don't mind. Let me carry on in my blissful ignorance.'

Similarly, when people behave under what is clearly and predictably in line with post-hypnotic suggestion, they typically are able to give quite rational explanations for their behaviour – explanations which have nothing to do with what everybody else in the room considers to be a predicted response determined by the actual cause. The hypnotist clicks his fingers and suddenly the subject goes over and opens the window. When asked to explain this, rationalisations, which the subject believes to be reasons, are offered. What the subject takes to be freely produced behaviour, everyone else in the audience knows to be the result of hypnotic suggestion. Again, feeling free and actually being free are not the same thing at all.

Again, the uncompromising determinist would argue that all that there is to freedom is the feeling, or the illusion, that we are free. Moreover, that when you claim that you *will* to do X as opposed to Y, what you really mean is that at best you are providing post hoc rationalisations, i.e. reasons presented or constructed *after* the event, to explain to others, and importantly to yourself, the reasons that you actually behaved this way rather than in that way. After the event of making a choice or behaving in a particular way, you then look for rational and plausible explanations that you then tend to shroud within the mysterious construct of the will.

The hard line determinist would dismiss the construct of the will by asking the tricky question: 'What exactly is it, then, that does the willing?'

What does the willing?

To return, briefly, to the example concerning the behaviour of light as it passes, say, from air to water. It is known that the law of refraction is always in place. Light isn't able to stop in its tracks, assess the situation and then somehow *will* itself to bend at an angle not determined by the known refractive index. The behaviour of the light is lawful and determined. The route taken by the light is determined by the medium it is travelling to and from. Its behaviour is thus determined. So what is so special about human behaviour? The determinist would claim that it is just that human behaviour is the result of a far more complex set of determining factors. Some of these factors might in fact be unknown. But that behaviour is determined nonetheless. Determinism, moreover, would claim that the notion of free will is nothing more than an illusory construct. If free will is just an illusion, then it is an error to suggest that this thing called free will can actually do any willing at all. So why has this notion been invented? Perhaps this is best explained by contrasting *descriptive laws* with *prescriptive laws*. This contrast is explained in some detail later in the present chapter and also in Chapter Five.

The construct of free will

Descriptive laws outline the way that the world is. The predictable way that, for example, objects in the world obey the law of gravity. In psychology a variety of laws have been proposed. For example, Thorndike's (1911) *law of effect* (see p. 129). *Weber's Law* established that for each of the senses, discrimination between two stimuli was sensitive in a predictable and constant manner. Moreover that this constant varied consistently across each of the senses. Vision being the most sensitive, followed by perception of pain, then pitch, then taste, etc. Thus, precise statements were made which linked the physical and the psychological realms in terms of predictable and testable lawful relationships. Wertheimer (1923) discovered a variety of laws which govern our perception of visual stimuli: (a) proximity (b) similarity (c) closure and (d) Prägnanz (see below), to name only four of an eventual 114 that were established (Helson, 1933). Again, the physical world of visual stimuli is linked lawfully with what happens at the experiential/psychological level of perception. The *Law of Prägnanz* for example, suggests that we tend to perceive that which is the simplest and that which is also easiest verbally to describe. Kanizsa's triangle (Figure 6.2) is a good example of this. It is easiest to describe this as three black circles which are partially covered by an overlying white triangle which lies over and partially covers a black-rimmed triangle.

Come up with an alternative verbal description of Figure 6.2. Is the alternative more complex? And indeed not actually what you tend to perceive? Do you agree that this perceptual phenomenon is sufficiently convincing as a psychological law?

Thus, just as no one has to tell you to obey the laws of gravity (indeed such a command would be immediately seen as nonsensical), similarly, laws in psychology suggest that we do not have to be ordered to have less sensitive discriminative sensory powers for taste than for vision. Nor that we have to perceive Kanizsa's triangle in the way that we do. For these are descriptive laws which outline the way that the psychological world actually works.

Psychology, science and free will

It should be quite apparent at this point that the argument seems to have shifted somewhat from discussing free will to examining whether or not psychology can be considered to be a science, in the way that, say, biology and physics would claim to be. But if we can establish that there do indeed exist lawful relationships within psychology – that behaviour X is caused by event Y; that sensory experience A is always, or at the very least, generally, a result of stimulus B, etc. – then doesn't this really amount to claiming that the psychological world is a world of cause-and-effect? That, if we know the input – the environment that we put our participants into – then we can predict the output – their behavioural response, etc. Hence, if we can claim that such causal relationships indeed do exist, isn't there a strong case for claiming that human behaviour and experience are determined and predictable, and, importantly, for being able to claim that we are determined and not as free as we tend to think ourselves to be? Is it not in fact the case that our introspective account of ourselves, the *feeling* that we are free, is faulty and illusory?

Is our behaviour determined and predictable?

(a) Just being human is a constraint on freedom

A great deal of energy has, of course, gone into trying to formalise the world of human behaviour and experience, that is, into attempting to describe under what circumstances people will behave in one way rather than another. What sorts of things will cause people to hold particular beliefs? The thousands of texts and journal articles written by psychologists are testimony to these attempts. In cognitive psychology, where the focus is upon how we process information, experimental evidence supports the proposal that universal principles exist. For example, one principle is that perception is driven by what are called *bottom-up processes*, those driven by the actual visual data/input itself, and also that *top-down processes* are involved, in that beliefs and expectations about stimuli are important factors contributing to what we actually come to perceive (Gregory, 1966, 1970). Studies of memory have indicated that the capacity of short-term memory is about seven items, irrespective of how much information is actually contained within the items (Miller, 1956). Hence, it is probably reasonable to conclude that one of the limits to our freedom is that we are contained within the *limits* of the biological system that we have inherited. Whether or not we *will* ourselves to, we are not free to fly through the air. Similarly, we are subject to the known principles of information-processing. Under normal circumstances, for example, we are not able to recall more than about seven or eight items from short-term memory. To make the point concerning these biological constraints may seem at first sight to be rather trivial or silly. However, the constraints of the sensory system actually determine our *being in* and hence *knowledge of* the world. Along these lines, the philosopher Immanuel Kant proposed that we can never really *know* the world. We can only know the world as it is 'filtered', so to speak, through our senses. Humans 'know' the world mainly through the sense of vision, bats through sonar. What we know about the world, and how we know it, are determined by what kind of animal we are. There are, then, very real constraints in place by the very fact of being human, of having this particular biology. This, of course, concerns humanity as a whole. These are aspects which are common to us all. In contrast, the section below on biological determinism looks at the way in which it might be argued that biological inheritance can determine **individual differences** amongst humans.

(b) Biological determinism

When we see someone who seems to be behaving freely, the strict behaviourist would say that this is only how things appear to us. We are, after all, not aware of the other person's reinforcement history. So, how do we know that the behaviour is freely produced? We do not know in what way this person has been reinforced for exhibiting certain behaviours (which we see at this point in time as apparently 'freely' produced); nor do we know what behaviours not presently exhibited are simply absent because they have been punished or ignored by others in the past. It might similarly be tempting to conclude that a person is extrovert (that is out-going and seeking stimulation) or that a person is introvert (inward-looking and generally tending to avoid stimulation) simply because that is what they choose to do. Perhaps it is tempting to conclude that the difference between the extravert and the introvert is the result of individual choice. Although we know well what the behaviourist would have to say about this, the individual concerned may assert that their tendency to introversion or to extraversion is a function of their will. But what about the biological causes of behaviour? After all, it is only logical to suppose that all behaviour has a biological origin. For example the hypothalamus, which is a relatively small part of the brain considering its apparent functions, has a controlling role in, amongst other things, the body's thermostat or heat control; water and food intake; sex drive; and aggression responses. The cerebellum is involved in fine movements and balance. Language functioning is located, predominantly, in the left cerebral hemisphere: Broca's area seems to control speech production, Wernicke's area controls the comprehension of speech, and so on. We cannot get away from the simple fact that, to put it crudely, no brain, no behaviour and no experience. All the willing in the world is not going to help someone with damage to Broca's area *tell* you just how free they feel.

Biological determinants of extraversion and introversion

So, is the behaviour of the extravert or introvert really a product of wilful tendencies? Indeed, extraverts will probably tell you that the way that they behave is the way that they wish to behave. Introverts will similarly be likely to explain their preference for peace and quiet as being chosen. In other words, a result of their own desires. Surely a clear-cut case of free will in operation if ever there was one. However, Gale (1979) provides experimental evidence that extraverts tend to have an under-aroused cerebral cortex (as measured by **EEG**), and that introverts tend to be over-aroused. Gale's explanation, then, for the behaviour of these personality types is that the extravert, by seeking out stimulation, is attempting to 'push up' the arousal level to within a (proposed) 'optimum level'. Introverts, by contrast, avoid stimulation in order to 'push down' an already over-aroused nervous system. Thus, what might appear to be freely chosen behaviour is in fact the result of biological factors over which we have no control.

The role of hormones

The role of hormones must also be considered. An example should illustrate the possible determining effects of hormones. This example concerns sexual orientation. In the 1950s and early 1960s many pregnant women took a synthetic form of the hormone estrogen in order to prevent miscarriage or to treat other pregnancy-related problems. Such hormones were known to produce masculinising effects upon the foetus similar to those related to testosterone. One study (Meyer-Bahlburg et al., 1995) found that seven out of 30 adult women whose mothers had taken synthetic estrogen reported some degree of homosexual or bisexual interest. This compared to a control group of 30 women who had not been exposed *in utero* to synthetic estrogen. In the control group, only one woman reported same-sex interest. This research provides some evidence to suggest that sexual preference may not necessarily be the result of 'free choice', but rather that it may be the product of determining effects of the developing child's environment. This example illustrates the possible role of hormones in determining sexual preference and behaviour. It also serves as a reminder that the effects of the environment – nurture – considered in Chapter Six must include a consideration of the individual's environment in the womb. An article covering similar research to the one described above is outlined in detail in Chapter Eight.

Behavioural ecology

The biological origin of what appears to be freely exhibited behaviour is also emphasised by those working within the domain of **behavioural ecology**. This approach proposes that the sole, or at least ultimate, purpose of all of our behaviour is quite simply to pass on our genes, to reproduce and, importantly, to ensure the survival of our offspring. This biologically-driven imperative underlies all of our behaviour. Researchers in this field often draw upon the behaviour of other species to make their point. Here is an extract from Ridley (1994), where he describes the efforts of male birds to ensure that the offspring produced by their mates are indeed carrying their genes and not those of another male:

> . . . much of the behaviour of male birds can be explained on the assumption that they are in constant terror of their wives' infidelity. Their first strategy is to guard the wife during the period when she is fertile . . . They follow them everywhere, so that a female bird who is building a nest is often accompanied on every trip by a male who never lends a hand: he just watches. The moment she has finished laying the clutch of eggs, he relaxes his vigil and begins himself to seek adulterous opportunities.

And later discussing the behaviour of swallows:

> If the pair has just been reunited after a separation or if a strange male intrudes into his territory and is chased out, the husband

will often copulate with the wife immediately afterwards, as if to ensure that his sperm are there to compete with the intruder's. (Ridley, 1994, p. 219)

In the above extracts it is clear that the male bird's behaviour is altogether selfishly concerned with the survival of his own genes. It must be stressed that this behaviour is certainly not driven by what might be called free will. Rather, it is simply guided by a 'blind' genetically encoded 'command' to reproduce. Or, more basically, to pass on genes. With respect to human sexual behaviour, Baker (1999) outlines anthropological studies of some South American societies where the belief in shared biological paternity dictates that:

> ... the number of fathers a baby has depends on how free the woman was with her favours over the preceding months. The man with whom she had most sex and who thus contributed most semen to the baby's body is the primary father, the second most favoured male its secondary father and so on. When a woman gives birth among the Bar of Venezuela and Colombia she publicly names all the men with whom she had intercourse during pregnancy. . . . All of these secondary fathers have recognised obligations to the child.

Baker points out that detailed studies of the Bar society indicate that some 24 per cent of children had, so to speak, 'multiple fathers'. Amongst the Ach of Paraguay, the figure is 63 per cent. The important point here is understanding the mother's promiscuity in terms of the biological imperative to further her genetic endowment. That is, to find a means of passing on her genes. According to the behavioural ecologist's perspective, this is our only real, ultimate purpose in life. The benefits for the woman, then, are summed up as follows:

> Among the Bar, for example, a pregnant woman who has a lover as well as a husband runs a lower risk of miscarriage and of the baby dying at birth. This is probably because her lover gives her gifts of fish and game during pregnancy, keeping her better fed and healthier. The resulting child will also have a higher chance of survival to age 15 years (80 per cent as against 64 per cent)

because it will be supported by two fathers. The incentive for a prospective mother is clear: promiscuity can improve her child's prospects.

To place a quite straightforward interpretation on the above, it can be seen that the cultural acceptance of promiscuity amongst the Bar and the Ach is a clear-cut case of cultural belief driving sexual behaviour. For the woman, however, the rather more 'hidden' imperative for her to pass on her genes is certainly served by this cultural set-up. The men involved believe themselves to have at least some pay-off in terms of this imperative.

Men and women from the Bar and the Ach would be unlikely to offer these sorts of explanations. People generally, whether from South America or Europe, will tend to introspect upon their own behaviour and offer explanations relating to free will, rather than explanations based upon anthropological and genetic arguments.

(c) The determining effects of others

Experimental social psychology has provided a variety of **replicable** phenomena. These include the observed experimental findings that people in larger groups tend to come to 'riskier' decisions than people working in smaller groups (Stoner, 1961). Milgram (1963) demonstrated the behavioural effects of the presence of a malevolent authority figure. Zajonc (1965) examined the effects of the presence of others and found that participants performed more efficiently at tasks that they were already proficient in and that they learned new tasks more slowly in the presence of an audience. Observational studies in the 'real' world have provided evidence, for example, that generally drivers will exceed the speed limits depending upon a variety of factors. In fact, this evidence suggests that it is possible to predict with some confidence that males are more likely to exceed the speed limit; that younger drivers are more likely to do so; that the speed limit tends to be exceeded when driving alone; and that this is also the case when driving along an often-repeated route (Lawrence, 1999). In terms of examining the effects of others upon behaviour, the evidence presented by Lawrence here underlines the effects of the presence or absence of passengers on driving behaviour. As such, there is a clear indication that the driving speed of an individual is determined not so much by personal choice or free will but rather that this is a relatively predictable result of cause–effect factors.

(d) A comparative approach

It could be argued that within the framework of behaviourism, psychology had to go a long way down the **phylogenetic** scale to establish mechanistic cause–effect relationships. Does this, however, imply that when it comes to humans such deterministic causality is not present? Or does it simply suggest that the determining factors of human behaviour are so complex and numerous that it is not possible to map them all out? Behaviourism provided a framework within which it was possible to predict and control the behaviour of lower animals. Indeed this control over behaviour was quite remarkable at times. Skinner (1960), for example, describes his success in training pigeons through operant conditioning techniques to guide missiles onto enemy warships. However, Watson's (1924) claim (see pp. 130–131) that *in principle* and given the right environmental set-up, he could produce a beggarman or a thief out of any healthy infant, remains an empty boast given the practical and ethical impossibility of such a venture.

Ethological studies

The study of animals in their natural environment has provided a sharp focus as to just how genuinely mechanistic animal behaviour can seem to be. (For example, Tinbergen, 1951; Lorenz, 1966.) There are countless examples. The greylag goose's egg-rolling behaviour is often provided as a good illustration of what is undoubtedly a hard-wired instinctive and mechanical behavioural response to the environment. The goose will always retrieve an egg that has rolled away from the nest in exactly the same manner. That is, the goose's behaviour is *stereotyped*; it is universal to the species – all greylag geese exhibit exactly the same response; the behaviour is described as *ballistic* – meaning that, once the behavioural response is set in motion, it will continue until the behavioural pattern is complete; and the behaviour is only released by a specific stimulus – in this case an egg. The behaviour pattern is only exhibited for this function of retrieving an egg.

Clearly, then, human behaviour is less rigid than that described above. It is clearly more complex and unlike the greylag goose's behaviour it can be changed as a function of learning. But does this mean that human behaviour is any less determined? Are we simply concerned here with relative complexity? Furthermore, just because human behaviour would seem to be much more an end-product of the environmental factors proposed by learning theorists, does this not still rob us of free will? The chapters presented in this text on the nature–nurture question (Chapter Six) and on behaviourism (Chapter Seven) go some way to attempting to answer these questions.

Free will and responsibility

The argument has been presented concerning the attempts of psychologists to uncover the naturally-occurring (descriptive) laws that govern human behaviour and experience. In order to pursue the issue concerning the relationship between free will and responsibility, it is necessary to consider another set of laws: prescriptive laws.

Prescriptive laws

Prescriptive laws are human rather than natural products. They do not describe the world as it is. Rather they describe the world as those creating such laws would have it be. Thus, the command 'thou shalt not kill' is not a description of what goes on in the world. Nor is it a prediction about what you are necessarily going to do or what you are not going to do. For many people do get killed at the hands of others. Hence, human laws are prescriptive, rather than descriptive. But how do these prescriptive laws fit in within the argument concerning free will? More specifically how does the idea of free will tie in with the notion of personal responsibility? If free will is just a construct rather than a fact, is it really fair to hold people responsible for what they do?

Well, the answer to this might be quite simple. Imagine that you do something to me that I don't like. It may or may not be something that is against the law. Even if I am a die-hard determinist and believe that you couldn't help doing what you did, am I not likely to punish you or respond in some manner that is going to stop you from doing whatever you did again, if only to determine your future behaviour, or simply just to make myself feel better for having retaliated? But whatever retaliation or punishment I might hand out, is this not also just a determined effect in response to your behaviour? Notions of free will don't necessarily come into the equation here, despite the fact that I might feel that I am freely attempting to shape your future behaviour.

Feeling free and being free

The argument that there is a real difference between feeling free and actually being free has already been touched upon. Most psychologists would probably agree that, when it comes to **introspection**, we are not always very good at explaining or knowing the causes of our own behaviour. Freud, of course, painted a picture of human psychology wherein the super-ego was in constant battle in pushing down the unacceptable and usually sexual drives of the id into the unconscious. Here, they would 'lurk around', so to speak, occasionally emerging into conscious life in a symbolic (and hence not immediately consciously recognisable) form. Alternatively, they would appear in disguised dream states in symbolic imagery, or these wishes and desires, which unknown to ourselves were driving our behaviour and motivation, would emerge in the form of so-called Freudian slips.

Freud wrote about unconscious desires as opposed to free will driving our behaviour. Therapy might often involve providing the patient with the opportunity to uncover such (often destructive) desires. Hence, a woman who repeatedly gets involved with violent men who abuse her might usefully discover in therapy that she is unconsciously seeking out men whose behaviour is similar to the way her own violent father treated her mother. Stopping such a cycle of abuse, then, could only come about by confronting this unconsciously-driven need to replace her father.

If you are not aware of what you are doing or why you are doing it, how can you be said to be acting freely? Freud's proposal of the unconscious, then, suggested a metaphorical 'blindness' to an individual's own underlying motives.

Free will and causation: 'bottom-up' and 'top-down' causation

With respect to physical determinism, the line of argument is outlined below and would seem to be quite straightforward:

1. Every macroscopic physical event has a cause;
2. every human action is a macroscopic event;

3. therefore, every human action is caused;
4. any event that is caused could not have happened otherwise than it did;
5. therefore, no human action could have happened otherwise than it did.

(From O'Connor, 1971)

Searle examines the idea of bottom-up and top-down causation thus:

So, for example, suppose I wish to cause the release of the neurotransmitter acetylcholine at the axon end-plates of my motorneurons. I can do it by simply deciding to raise my arm and then raising it. Here, the mental event, the intention to raise my arm, causes the physical event, the release of acetylcholine – a case of top-down causation if ever there was one. . . . But top-down causation only works because the top level is already caused by and realised in the bottom levels. (Searle, 1991, pp. 93–94)

Searle's point here is that what looks like top-down/macro causation – deciding to do something which causes effects at the microscopic levels – is indeed top-down as far as the release of acetylcholine at the axon end-plates is concerned. However, this decision must itself also be caused by events at the bottom levels. When we make a decision, it may feel as though we've just decided and that's all that there is to it, but, this would simply be to side-step the issue of how decisions are inevitably the end-result of neurological events at the 'bottom' level.

If that's the way that things happen, then, it's not difficult to come to the conclusion that no thought or decision, and in turn, no voluntary action, could be caused by anything other than these kinds of biological events. It is thus difficult to conclude that there could ever be any kind of causation as a function of what we so casually term 'free will'. Again, we come back to the idea that free will is nothing more than a construct, or a way of talking which we feel ourselves to have, but which in fact has nothing at all to do with the way things really happen.

Existentialism

Existentialism is a branch of philosophy which insists that humans are *in* the world, rather than simply a part *of* it. This really implies that humans are in some way rather special in that they have what is called *agency*. In other words, they are free agents and act upon the world, rather than merely react mechanistically within it. Sartre (1946) explains this idea with the assertion that 'existence precedes essence'. Now the word 'essence' has its root in the Latin word 'esse' which means 'to be'. Sartre's argument is that some things in the world don't come into being until they have first existed as an idea in the mind of a conscious individual. As such, these things are freely created. The striking example that he gives of this is the way in which an everyday article such as a penknife comes into being. The way in which it can actually become to be there in front of you to see or to use. His argument is that it would be very strange for the person completing the manufacture of the penknife (perhaps after several days of cutting away at the bits of wood and metal from which the eventual object is composed) to declare 'Oh! that looks nice. I wonder what it could be used for? What on earth is that for?' Clearly such a declaration would be ridiculous because the finished object had already existed as an idea in the mind of the designer producing it, and it had been designed according to plans connected with its proposed use. Its form was directed and dictated by the use to which it was intended. It should be clear at this point that here is an object brought *to* the world by human design and wilful intention. Rather different from those things in the world that simply *are*, such as a rock, the ocean or a cloud.

Sartre takes this argument a little further by suggesting that the person that any individual eventually becomes is the end-product of a similarly wilful – free – act. In order to make this point, Sartre (1943) describes an 'over-acting waiter'. This is an individual who 'pours himself into' the prescribed or ready-made social role of what a waiter is supposed to be and how a waiter is required to act. The central idea to existential freedom is, to use Sartre's slogan, that we are 'condemned to freedom'. And Sartre would insist that this freedom is born out of the fact that we are first of all nothing and that we become whatever we choose to make of ourselves. We are nothing but our own project. However, Sartre's waiter refuses to accept the responsibility that this initial nothingness and hence freedom brings:

> All the movements and gestures of the waiter are slightly over-done. His behaviour is essentially ritualistic. He bends forward in a manner which is too deeply expressive of concern and

deference for the diners; he balances his tray in a manner that is just a little too precarious. His movements are all of them like the movements in a mime or a game. The game which he is playing is the game of 'being a waiter'. He is quite consciously acting out the role of waiter, and executing the peculiar waiter's 'dance'. 'The waiter in the café plays with his condition in order to realize it.' He wishes, that is to say, to make his condition real, so that he shall have no choices left, but shall be completely and wholly absorbed in being a waiter. (Warnock, 1992, p. 103)

Conclusions concerning Sartre's ideas on freedom

Freedom to choose what we are/what we become: In describing his 'over-acting' waiter, Sartre is clearly attempting to demonstrate to his readers that we are all potentially 'guilty' of acting out roles at the expense of freely expressing ourselves. Now, it must also be said that acting out roles is actually demanded within many social situations. For instance, a student of psychology is required to take on the student role. The teacher of psychology is also expected to behave in a particular manner – or at the very least within particular limits. When we approach a police officer for assistance, we expect – perhaps even *demand* – that the response we get is within the role of a police officer.

Taking on such roles doesn't necessarily mean that a person is guilty of refusing to act freely. But Sartre's objection here is that his 'over-acting waiter' refuses to be anything other than his prescribed role. In other words, Sartre's waiter chooses to be nothing more than a waiter. That is to say, the waiter takes his role much too seriously and seems to have lost sight that all he is really doing is acting out a role. In taking this role too seriously, this waiter is avoiding the responsibility of making any choices for himself. He is refusing to act freely, and he does this by becoming totally absorbed in being a waiter. According to Sartre, this is a strategy that many people can be tempted to employ in order to avoid the 'burden of freedom' that is the lot of human beings.

Sartre's views on the question of whether or not we are free are really not that complicated at all. Unlike the stereotyped behaviour of the greylag goose (see the section Ethological studies), human beings would seem to have much more choice in terms of how they behave. Because of our mental capacities, we are able to plan ahead, to work towards projects of our own design, to create. In fact, Sartre insists, we are capable of making real choices concerning what we 'make of ourselves'.

Summary

This chapter has provided quite a lot of material which challenges our common-sense views concerning free will. Perhaps much of what is presented here seems to be in favour of the idea that we human beings are determined by forces beyond our own immediate control. Re-read Searle's argument, as presented in the section on Bottom-up and top-down causation. This is really quite compelling and is in fact central to the whole issue concerning free will. If we are just a collection of atoms, then everything we do and everything we think must surely just be the end-result of these atoms of which we are composed. Atoms which all obey the laws of physics. And if this is the case, then we must surely accept that we are determined by these atoms, and we must therefore reject the common-sense view that we are *self*-determining.

Arguments have also been presented in this chapter concerning the determining aspects of events outside of our own bodies. For example, we are social animals and hence are required to behave in terms of the demands of whatever social environment (group/s) we find ourselves in. Another brand of environmental determinism, of course, is behaviourism. This is dealt with at some length in Chapter Seven.

But we do *feel* that we are free, don't we? So the reader must reach his/her own conclusion concerning Sartre's insistence, as presented towards the end of the present chapter, that we are 'condemned to freedom'. It could be the case that Sartre might just be wrong to insist on this feeling of freedom.

Re-read the material in the section 'The determining effects of others' regarding driving behaviour (Lawrence, 1999). Now consider the following case:

Two drivers have just completed a journey across the same stretch of road. One is an 18-year-old man, travelling alone from his place of work to his home. The other is a woman of 35 travelling with a friend on her way to visit the dentist. One of the two drivers exceeded the speed limit whilst making this journey.

Review exercise

Now write down some answers to the following questions:

(a) Would you bet that it was the young man who exceeded the speed limit? Explain your answer.

(b) And if so, does this imply that his behaviour was determined? Again, write down a brief explanation for your answer to this question.

(c) Could he have willed himself to behave otherwise? Write down how you would *defend* your answer to this question.

(d) If the woman *did* keep within the speed limit, and the man did not, does this make her a 'better' person than the man? Write down how you would defend your answer to this question.

Further reading

Searle, J. (1991) *Minds, Brains & Science*, London: Penguin. Chapter 6: The freedom of the will. This is a readable and lively text. A second chapter from Searle's text is also suggested for further reading with reference to the mind–body debate.

Nagel, T. (1987) *What Does it All Mean? A Very Short Introduction to Philosophy*, Oxford: Oxford University Press. Chapter 6: Free will. An extremely clear text which presents arguments in a very chatty manner. Nagel has written this text in such a way that it can be understood without any prior knowledge of philosophy or psychology. A second chapter from this text is recommended with reference to the mind–body debate.

Hospers, J. (1990) *An Introduction to Philosophical Analysis*, 3rd edn, London: Routledge. Chapter 5: Cause, determinism and freedom.

Reductionism

Introduction

This chapter examines the idea that because the world and everything in it, including human beings, is made up of atoms and sub-atomic particles, then perhaps the best way to study psychology – human behaviour and experience – is from the bottom-up, so to speak. The 'reductionist' approach implies that for every thought that an individual has and for every behaviour that s/he exhibits, such thoughts and behaviours are undeniably 'created' out of and made possible by events at a 'lower' level. It's simply an undeniable fact that we as human beings are 'merely' an integrated biological system made up of atoms. It's just a fact that anything that can be talked about at 'higher' levels, such as a picnic, a car, a textbook, a table, a human being, or an idea, etc., is only possible because they emerge out of physical and biological matter composed of atoms. Chapter Four which examines the mind–body question continues this argument. Here the issue addressed is whether or not it is reasonable to suggest that when we talk about 'mind' we should be talking about something physical – made up of atoms – or *meta*-physical – somehow something *more* than mere matter. The present chapter also examines experimental reductionism and the implications of the evolutionary perspective.

Reductionism and levels of explanation

Consider, briefly, a simple behaviour like signing a cheque. There is no problem with that perhaps; signing a cheque is quite simple. Signing a cheque is signing a cheque. That's all that there is to it. Well, it is; but then again it isn't. Even something as simple as this can be described at a number of different levels, and that is where the problem arises. To make things clear, we will explore each of the possible different levels of explanation with regard to signing a cheque. It will be helpful to start at the bottom level – the most *reductionist* – and work upwards to the least reduced level – the most *holistic*.

Figure 3.1 shows the levels under consideration and where they are in the hierarchy. It should be noted that there may be other levels that could be placed between the ones chosen for this illustration. Likewise, there are levels below level (1) and above level (7), but these do not need to concern us now. The levels given in Figure 3.1, then, are sufficient here for gaining some appreciation of the principles involved.

(1) Neurological level

At the smallest unit level to be considered in this illustration, it could reasonably be stated that in order to sign a cheque, the writer's brain must be involved at some level. The hand movements don't just happen by themselves as a kind of random muscular activity. The hand receives instruction from the brain, and particularly from one part of the brain – the motor cortex. It works in conjunction with the cerebellum, the area of the brain known to be important in controlling intricate movement. Once an individual has developed a firmly adopted manner of signing their name, it is likely to be 'programmed' within this part

(7) sociological/political level	**Holistic**
(6) social-psychological level	⇓
(5) psychological level	⇓
(4) physical/muscular level	⇓
(3) physiological systems	⇓
(2) physiological units level	⇓
(1) neurological	⇓
	Reductionist

Figure 3.1 **Levels of explanation (adapted from Rose 1976)**

of the brain, and the act of signing then becomes rather automatically triggered from this area. The term 'programmed' in this context implies the idea that the pathways between the brain and the writing of a signature are very much in place, established and automatic. These pathways could be compared to the wiring in a house. The flick of a particular switch leads, for example, to a particular light coming on because the pathway is wired up and established.

(2) Physiological units level

Working up to the next higher level, it might be argued that it is not just the cerebellum and the motor cortex which are responsible for signing. This would not really make too much sense. Although these are necessary units for the signing of the cheque to be achieved, other physiological units contribute to the signing of the cheque. For example, the visual system would usually tend to be involved. Obviously, parts of the brain other than the cerebellum will also be involved. For example, the very decision to sign the cheque must originate within the brain somewhere. The whole business of hand–eye co-ordination would involve other parts of the brain, and so on. Indeed those researchers interested in reductionist explanations would ultimately need to be concerned with just how the different parts involved actually work together.

(3) Physiological systems level

So now it can be argued that it is an integration of the writer's entire physiologically inter-related system that is involved. It is the whole organism that does the writing. The term 'organism', of course, implies this sort of 'organisation'.

(4) Physical/muscular level

Of course, this is really the only level that the strict behaviourist would be interested in addressing. Physiological and biological aspects, so the behaviourist would argue, are for the realm of physiology and biology, not for psychology. The behaviourist approach, then, simply insists that only overt behaviour should be the data for psychology. At this level, then, what is available to the observer? Simply the movements of the writer's arm and hand as he exhibits cheque-signing behaviour: as simple as that. Whereas the other three levels are to be dismissed as being outside of the realm of psychology and more the concern of the biological sciences, the following higher levels, which are outlined in some detail below, are to be excluded because they are not readily observable. They are much less tangible (meaning that they cannot be directly touched), material, observable, and so on. The behavioural level concerns only that which is overt, i.e. openly observable.

There are many researchers, however, who argue that all of the questions that we ultimately wish to answer concerning psychology will eventually be explained by examining the more reductionist levels of physiology and biology, and that, having examined these levels, it would then be possible to put all the parts back together, so to speak. We would thereby arrive at an understanding that has been achieved by synthesising or re-building from the bottom up, that is from an understanding of the basic building blocks or the bottom levels, up to a detailed account of how the whole brain works.

(5) Psychological level

This, as with the next two higher levels, is rather less tangible or, it could be said, less immediately observable. Signing a cheque may involve a variety of psychological aspects which are not observable to others. But to the person actually writing the cheque these could be far more important than the behavioural level (4) above. Indeed, the actual act of signing may, for the writer, seem only a necessary vehicle for more important psychological realities. The writer of the cheque may at the psychological level feel or think a number of things which are unobservable to others. Such things could include: (a) pride, 'I seem to be coping well with my finances this month'; (b) resentment, 'I actually resent writing this cheque at all. Why should parents have to pay tuition fees to universities attended by their children?'; (c) anger, 'This parking fine is excessive for over-staying by just ten minutes.' The psychological level involves 'looking into' the head, so to speak, of the person writing the cheque and imagining the sorts of psychological realities that surround the behaviours involved in writing the cheque.

(6) Social-psychological level

However, humans are highly social animals. As such, the adoption of the purely behavioural level of explanation (as described in section (4) above) can be seen as trivialising what is actually going on. The invisible social strings of obligation to others etc. that underlie much of our behaviour cannot be denied. When I write a cheque, it can indeed be described as a series of arm and hand movements, muscle contractions, etc. However, to suggest that this is all I am doing when writing the cheque is absurd. For this behaviour can also be viewed within its social context. Hence I may be repaying a long-standing debt to a friend. As such the social-psychological context might transform this behavioural act into a much higher idea. For example, I am preserving my sense of honour in terms of dutifully repaying what is due. I am not just making arm movements, I am settling a debt. In this sense, then, it is perfectly reasonable to suggest that if I am asked what I am doing, the legitimate response to this would be, 'I am repaying a debt to a dear friend'. This is the appropriate level of explanation. The most appropriate account of what I am doing. Indeed, the person asking this question of me would be likely to be extremely offended if I were to reply 'I'm exhibiting behaviour mainly consisting of arm movements. Why do you ask? Is it not obvious?' Indeed, such a reply would be taken as sarcasm. Furthermore, should the question actually come from the friend to whom the money is owed, then such a reply would be clearly unsatisfactory because it bypasses the reality of what really is going on at the social, interpersonal level.

Thus it might be claimed that the social context within which behaviour occurs is of great importance and that to focus merely upon the observable behaviour exhibited is an unacceptable and rather blinkered form of reductionism. It is also one which loses sight of the fact that much of our openly observable behaviour has social implications that are less immediately visible. These social implications are, however, very real. The behaviour of an individual is often of significance to others.

Consider the fact that bees, upon re-entering the hive, exhibit a particular kind of dance in a figure eight. It turns out that the angle at which the figure eight dance is performed in relation to the hive itself signifies to other bees just where the nectar is located outside of the hive. The speed of the wing movements is also significant in that it provides information concerning the distance of the nectar source from the hive. Thus it is evident that the bee's dance must not be seen in isolation, but rather it can only be properly understood within the context of what it conveys to other bees. Hence, to concentrate upon the individual bee would be an unhelpfully reduced account which ignores the wider social purpose of the behaviour under scrutiny.

Returning to human behaviour, it could similarly be argued that squeezing the index finger on the trigger of a gun needs to be viewed in terms of the social context within which this behaviour is exhibited. The problem, otherwise, is that this piece of behaviour can be exhibited in a variety of very different social contexts. The act of firing the gun might result in a court case, an Olympic Gold Medal, or a rabbit stew for a farmer's family meal. Reduction to the behaviour level – whilst ignoring the intention behind the behaviour – is, again, unhelpful and incomplete.

(7) Sociological/political level

Returning to the illustration concerning the signing of a cheque, this might be viewed within the context of its social, sociological and political significance. Thus it is not simply *about* signing a cheque, nor is the act of signing merely symbolic, for it can achieve an end-goal. Signing might actually be part of a necessary banking mechanism for transferring large amounts of money from one account to another or from one place to another. Perhaps, similar to the above example of firing a gun, the act of signing a cheque may involve similar muscular movements and arm-moving behaviour to writing a shopping list, but the significance and effect might be much more far-reaching. Vast amounts of much-needed money might thereby be transferred to a poor country. Here the writer is doing more or less the same thing in behavioural terms as an international footballer is doing when signing an autograph for an adoring fan, but signing an autograph and transferring money are very different things. Again, the idea of the intrinsic meaning behind the behaviour is very important. The problems inherent in referring to this merely as a behavioural account, whilst ignoring the higher levels, social, sociological and political, are examined next.

Strengths and weaknesses of behavioural accounts

The Prime Minister, Neville Chamberlain, returned from Munich on September 30, 1938 with a signed agreement from Adolf Hitler and the famous assertion, 'I believe it is peace for our time'. The following year marked the start of the Second World War following Russia and Germany's invasion of Poland. Whether or not he actually did, Hitler is reputed to have reduced the status, effect, promise and significance of this 'agreement' saying, 'Well, he seemed such a nice man, I thought I'd give him my autograph.' The problem with accounts which bypass 'higher' levels of explanation is again all too apparent. Such accounts are indeed unacceptably reduced. There is an obvious difference between giving someone your autograph and giving them a promise of world peace, although, at the behavioural level, both involve the same observable hand movements when the paper is signed.

Political and social context, social obligations, etc. are not as readily observable as the actual act of signing a cheque. Hitler's sarcastic comment mentioned above points to that which is undeniable to any observer. It points to the obvious hand movements associated with writing an autograph or signing a cheque but not to the rather more hidden intentions of the writer. This is perhaps both a strength and a weakness of the behavioural level of explanation. A strength because we can be very sure about the behavioural level of description, and a weakness because other less easily visible realities have been ignored.

One area of philosophy is concerned with **epistemology**. This word simply refers to how we come to know anything, and how we know whether what we know is actually true. Hence, the behavioural level of description could be said to be epistemologically sound. It is indisputable that hand movements are being made. However, there are weaknesses associated with the behavioural level of explanation. One such weakness is related to the problem of explaining long-term goals within the framework of behaviourism, and this is addressed in the following section.

Explanations of behaviour in terms of long-term goals

It is important that the on-going context is considered when accounting for behaviour. Should a snapshot be taken of behaviour at one point in time, it would not provide a very satisfactory explanation of what is really going on. Consider, for example, a child tying a pair of shoe-laces. The end-result of having properly tied laces may be only one sub-goal in a series of sub-goals that are necessary for achieving an overall aim or goal. Thus, the overall aim of the child might be to get ready for school, of which tying laces is but one small part. If the child were to be asked 'what are you doing?', a legitimate response would be for the child to describe the sub-goal, hence the reply 'I'm tying my shoe-laces'. However, this may be received as sarcasm, for the fact that shoe-laces are being tied is evident to any onlooker. A more likely reply would represent the overall goal, not this necessary step on the way, or sub-goal. Hence, 'I'm getting ready for school' would be more likely. Similarly, should a parent tell the child to get ready for school, it would be odd for the parent to get irate should the child's response be to start tying shoe-laces. The response, 'I asked you to get ready for school, not to start messing around with bits of string', would be to ignore the overall context within which this behaviour needs to be viewed.

Explanation of phenomena with reference to ultimate goals or purpose is often referred to as *teleology*. This is from the Greek word *tele* which simply means distance or far. Hence the word television represents the idea of seeing things from far away. Similar roots underlie the words telephone and telepathy. Teleological explanations of behaviour are those which address the end goals of behaviours, not just the snapshot of one piece of behaviour frozen in time and devoid of context. Here, then, the problem for behaviourism should be quite evident. If the strength of behaviourism was to be that only overt, publicly available, undeniable behaviour should be the data for analysis, then surely purposive behaviour presents a difficulty. Many ultimate end goals require the individual to exhibit behaviour over a long period of time. The end goals of behaviour are not always there in front of the observer to see, and the example above of the child getting ready for school illustrates this. All behaviour, then, needs to be accounted for sensibly within its context. Again, this is the unfortunate tendency of behaviourism to reduce the account from an on-going purposive set of behavioural subroutines (which have an end goal in sight) to units of behaviour devoid of such purpose, meaning and context. As has been addressed above, this context includes not just the social meaning of behaviour, but also the on-going context of purpose. That is, teleological explanations are required.

Reductionism and the interpretation of social behaviour

The central idea of behaviourism is that only observable behaviour should form the basis of psychology because such data are more scientific/objective, etc. In the case of Skinner's work, the rat either pressed the bar and obtained food, or it didn't. It was observed to do so a particular and quantifiable number of times. It was also observed that different schedules of reinforcement produced differences in the rat's persistence in bar-pressing in the absence of reinforcement. But human behaviour, particularly human social behaviour, is a rather more complex business. Even simple everyday activities become problematic when the psychologist attempts to account for them. Hence, it might be argued that behaviourism is an inappropriate kind of reductionism for psychology, and that it is inappropriate for several reasons. Notably, it could be argued that psychology had to go a long way down the phylogenetic scale – by examining the behaviour of rats and pigeons, for example – to establish a mechanistic account of behaviour. Thus, much was learned about rats and pigeons but little about humans. Behaviourists would argue that it is only by examining relatively simple animals that it is possible to tease out the basic principles which govern animal and hence human behaviour. Much in the same way perhaps that when scientists are developing aircraft, they adopt a reductionist approach by testing small-scale models of aircraft in small-scale environments such as wind tunnels. Under these reduced laboratory conditions, they would argue that it is possible to gain an understanding of how particular designs will stand up to a variety of flying conditions. They are then able to make fine adjustments to the final design of the aircraft.

But the above defence of the reductionist approach could easily be counter-attacked as follows: unlike this example where scaled-down models of the very item under investigation are used, rats and pigeons are not in any way scaled-down humans. A rat lives its life as a rat, and humans live their lives as humans. Thus, if you really wish to examine human behaviour, your starting point must surely be to stop treating human beings as if they were something else. Rom Harré, in fact, made a very simple suggestion (Harré and Secord, 1972). This suggestion was that it was time that psychologists starting treating human beings 'as if they were human'. At this point it might be appropriate to try to tease out what Harré really meant by using this slogan. Human beings are highly social animals. As such, their lives are lived according to highly complex factors. Thus, social rules, expectations, obligations and all the tricky aspects of what it is to live life as a human being need to be accounted for if we are really interested in establishing a psychology which has anything at all to do with real people. These aspects are referred to here as being 'tricky' because, as shall be outlined in the following section, they are not easy to examine or observe: they are rather more hidden, and hence difficult to examine objectively. So, what are these hidden rules that underpin human behaviour? The next section briefly touches upon this difficult, or tricky, domain.

Treating people as if they are human

This section focuses upon the limitations and problems associated with experimental reductionism in social psychology. The importance of 'mere' common sense is examined.

A branch of sociology which was very popular in the 1970s was **ethnomethodology**. This was generally concerned with accounting for those seen-but-unnoticed aspects of everyday social life, involving those rules that are taken for granted and background expectations of day-to-day living. The social scientists working within this domain were interested in unearthing these rules and expectations.

But why did they need to make them evident if everyone in everyday life was actually behaving according to the rules? The answer to this was that it is precisely because they are so well established and incorporated into much of our social behaviour in a rather automatic fashion that those following such rules, and having particular expectations, didn't even notice them.

These rules and expectations tend to be implicitly understood by people, rather than explicitly stated. That is, they tend to be dutifully followed without having to be formally, explicitly, stated or written down. Everybody somehow knows what these rules are.

Much of the work in *ethnomethodology* was by definition very commonplace. It examined ordinary aspects of everyday life. A typical example of this would be our behaviour when entering a café. Imagine that there is only one person in the café when you arrive. Where do you sit? What are the 'rules'? You may reply that there are no rules, none written down explicitly anyway. But what if I then suggest that you sit on the seat directly next to the other person in the café? Your reply is likely to be, 'But everybody knows that you shouldn't do that. It would be expected that I sit at a reasonable distance from the other person.' This reply, then, now makes explicit the 'rule' to follow and what the expectation would be.

The following is typical of the sort of work done in *ethnomethodology*. Again, it involves a commonplace scenario. Here a very basic behaviour (walking down the street) is examined. What are the 'rules' which allow us to interpret whether people are walking together, or walking alone? 'A child walking ten feet ahead of an adult woman may be seeable as mother-and-child, and thereby can be taken as walking-together, whereas a uniformed policeman and teenage girl walking in a similar arrangement may present us with no recognisable togethering-set, and each thereby can be taken as walking alone' (Ryave and Schenkein, 1974).

It is only once an attempt is made to write down formally and explicitly such rules that it becomes apparent just how many rules govern our behaviour and the interpretation of others' behaviour in everyday life. Everybody somehow knows that the woman and child are walking together, and this is because everybody is carrying around with them a vast amount of common-sense knowledge about the world. (In cognitive psychology such knowledge would be referred to as schemas.) Small children need to be supervised when walking in the street, but a policeman in uniform is on duty and hence cannot (or should not) be walking along with his girl-friend.

Social behaviour then cannot simply be measured in the true behaviourist manner. In other words, it cannot be *reduced down* to an analysis of the behaviour alone: the behaviour requires *interpretation*. This interpretation is governed by the vast amount of common-sense, taken-for-granted, knowledge that all members of a social group, or a particular society, possess.

Write down as many 'rules' and general expectations concerning behaviour that you can think of concerning the time of day or night that you would feel able to telephone the following: (a) a close friend; (b) a close relative; (c) the bank manager; (d) the doctor.

Reductionism and category errors

Many behaviours then can be explained at a variety of levels. The more reduced the account, generally speaking, the more readily available the 'proof' of our explanation would seem to be. There is something undeniable about readily observed behaviour. It would seem that biological 'realities' are of a rather different category than the realm of the psychological (level (5) in Figure 3.1). You cannot see, feel or touch the psychological. Only the person in a particular psychological state has direct knowledge of this realm. On the other hand, you can observe and measure exhibited behaviour. The realm of the biological world is similarly physical in nature. As such this physical world can be observed in a rather more direct manner by the scientist: action potentials can be measured; cells fire; EEGs can be employed to measure and record brain activity. On the contrary, levels (6) and (7) are particularly problematic. They concern 'realities' which simply do not yield themselves to such direct discrete, that is 'one-off', observation and measurement. The confusion of different levels of reality is really a form of **category error**.

This is rather similar to the story of the tourist asking to be shown around the University of Oxford. Having been shown many rooms, lecture theatres, etc., the tourist exclaimed 'Yes, but where is the University?' Hence the tourist is making a category error here. The reality of the institution is of a different category to particular rooms, etc. The institution, then, cannot be reduced down to particular rooms, etc. For the idea/reality of the University of Oxford exists at a higher category level than that at which particular observable rooms within it exist.

Category errors and the explanation of behaviour

This section briefly examines the philosophical idea of category error. Some behaviour, particularly social and interpersonal behaviour, simply doesn't present itself as being directly observable, that is, observed at one point in time. Consider the difference between (a) running for a bus and (b) running for President. One is discrete and the other is rather more complex and on-going in nature. The former can be observed 'in one sitting', so to speak. Running for President requires us to describe a multitude of behaviours as being part of the process of trying to get elected. If I describe Jim as running for President, you may well answer, 'but show me when and where he's doing just that'. The point is that I would only be able to give you examples of all the behaviours which, when added together, amount to what it is I claim Jim to be doing. Thus (a) and (b) are of two different categories. Running for a bus, however, can be more easily pinned down and then described.

Thus, it should similarly be apparent that within the realm of interpersonal behaviour, there is a difference in category between (a) hitting a colleague at work with a cricket bat and (b) thwarting the same colleague's chances of getting promotion. Again, the category difference should be obvious. In the case of (a), this is a readily observed piece of behaviour. What constitutes (a) is there in front of us to see. However, when asked for what constitutes (b), you are likely to be offered *examples* of such behaviour.

Similarly, the category difference between the following should be clear: (a) a man supporting his wife and children and (b) the very same man supporting the weight of his child on his knee. These clearly belong in different categories. Although logically possible, it is much more difficult to *reduce* what is required for (a) down to its component parts than it is for (b). As such, the reductionism associated with behavioural accounts is rather more problematic for (a). Again, this relates back to the discussion earlier in this chapter (pp. 40–41) regarding long-term goals.

Much of the discussion thus far concerning reductionism has focused upon levels of explanation. In particular, the focus has been on the strengths and weaknesses of the reductive aspects of behaviourism. There are, however, other important, related issues and kinds of reductionism. These will now be addressed. A separate chapter is devoted to the implications of reductionism for the mind–body problem.

Experimental reductionism

Trying to investigate the 'real world' is often very difficult because so many factors can influence what goes on in it. Often very many causes have many different effects all at once. In other words, so much is often going on that it is difficult to see exactly *what* is going on. It is for this reason that psychologists, and other scientists, of course, often prefer to create a 'smaller world' in the laboratory. They do this in order to focus specifically on one, or perhaps just a few, possible causes and effects. Thus many causes and effects are reduced to a manageable number. This is what is meant by *experimental reductionism*.

An example that illustrates and explains further what is meant by experimental reductionism could be that of a researcher attempting to identify the optimal size of a group for solving a problem. The participants might be randomly assigned to one of two experimental conditions. In the first condition, participants work within a small group of, say, three people. In the second condition, the group might consist of eight people. The speed with which the problem is solved under each condition can easily be measured. Thus, the only important factors here are (a) the size of the group and (b) the time taken to arrive at a solution. As the experimenter believes that the time taken to solve the problem might in some way be dependent upon the size of the group, (b) is referred to as the *dependent variable*. Whilst (a), of course, is the *independent variable*. The experimenter here might believe that the larger the group, then the longer it takes to reach a solution. A common-sense idea of 'too many cooks spoil the broth'. Alternatively, it might work the other way around. A larger group might be able to share ideas and pool resources. Another common-sense notion, but this time perhaps a case of 'many hands make light work'.

In defence of this kind of experimental investigation, it must first be said that the strength of empirical science is that, by conducting experiments, the researcher puts to one side a reliance on 'common-sense' knowledge about how the world works in favour of recording what actually happens when observations of the world itself are made. However, with the above example in mind, several criticisms of this type of experimental reductionism can be offered.

Some problems associated with experimental reductionism

(i) In order to allow subsequent replication, the experimenter needs to *operationalise* variables. The two important variables in the above example regarding group processes are clearly identified and easily operationalised. That is, easily and clearly defined in a manner which allows the researcher to operate. Now this seems to be quite straightforward. The time taken to solve the problem – the dependent variable – is particularly clear-cut. The stop-watch is started as the participants are given the problem to solve, and it is stopped when they reach the correct solution. Now, at first sight, it would seem that the size of the group – independent variable – is similarly clearly defined. Surely a group's size can be clearly defined and agreed upon, but as will now be explained, this is not always so straightforward.

Attempting to reduce the description of a group in this manner by counting the heads of the participants, so to speak, seems simple, objective and clearly defined. The experiment here suggests that a simple IV–DV (independent variable–dependent variable) relationship can be investigated. But simply counting heads (IV) and recording the length of time taken to solve the problem (DV) does not take into account what went on as the group were actually going about the business of solving the problem. This simple reduction of the variables into these quantities might, for example, miss the fact that the 'group' weren't much of a group at all. A group of eight such as this might have been too large for people to really work together. When the experimenter actually bothers to ask participants what was really going on within the group, quite frequently they report that the eight participants unofficially split into two smaller groups and that each group actually arrived at the correct solution independently. So, here, what at first sight looks like a group of eight, is actually two 'unofficial' groups of four.

Hence, this simple reduction of, in this case, the independent variable into a head count is a clear example of the way in which experimental investigations can only proceed by operationalising variables. This very act is an act of reduction to something which may well be measurable, but which bears no resemblance to what is actually going on within the experiment itself. The researcher's understanding is imposed at the expense of the participants' understanding of the situation. The researcher's point of view is that of an outsider. Whereas, inside the experiment itself, a completely different point of view would be available. But only if the researcher were to abandon this objective (but faulty) position in favour of the more subjective (but accurate) account that could be provided by the participants actually involved in the process.

(ii) Any overview of academic journals that cover this kind of experimental account of social processes will tend to reveal immediately that the sort of problem given to participants in this type of experiment is a form of reductionism in itself. In 'real life' institutional settings, for example, the problems presented are usually much more complex and ill-defined. In the desire that participants actually reach a solution during the experiment – hence providing a measure for the DV, in this case the solution time for the problem set – the problem presented will tend to have to be 'watered down' or at least be clearly solvable within a time-span that is realistic in terms of the experimental set-up itself.

(iii) Following on from the above point, it should be clear here that **internal validity** is achieved. That is, the experimenter is apparently clear about what variable is affecting what within the experiment itself. However, this is achieved at the expense of **external validity**, that is, at the expense of being able to realistically claim that the findings from this reduced experimental set-up can have any real relevance to what goes on in the 'real world'. Although by no means always the case, experimental social psychology of the sort described above has sometimes been criticised for concentrating upon relatively unimportant and trivial aspects of the social world. For example, how often eye contact is made when holding the floor during a conversation; how close people sit – or where exactly they choose to sit – during social interactions of various types, etc. Within this methodological exactitude, researchers could be accused of ignoring politically important social realities. Rather than reduce the social world to an experimental 'stage' for examining trivia, perhaps the social scientist should be involved in examining how the social world itself is created and maintained. It must be made clear that the sort of experimental reductionism just mentioned is not confined to social psychology. It must also be added that many researchers working within the domain of cognitive psychology would claim that experimental reductionism is a highly successful strategy for teasing out how the brain processes information. The issue of experimental reductionism in other areas of investigation in psychology is examined next.

Reductionism and the study of visual perception

Studies which are supposed to illustrate the principles of perception have been criticised for depending upon impoverished visual scenes, usually in the form of stylised two-dimensional 'tricks' or illusions such as the Müller-Lyer and the Necker Cube. Whilst these no doubt illustrate some of the principles which might be operating in perception, this preoccupation with reducing the study of perception to such visual rarities seems to avoid examining how we normally go about the business of making sense of the world. And, importantly, we see the world in three dimensions rather than two. This approach, apart from anything else, reduces its focus to an examination of perception as if it could be reduced to a few 'tricks', and as if it only involved the sense of vision. Now, this statement might seem, at first sight, to be rather strange. Surely, you might argue, it is the sense of vision that is under discussion here: what else should be the focus of discussion?

But the point here is that it could be argued that it is the *whole person*, not just the visual system, that is involved in the act of perception. For example, when you look at a violin, do you really just *see* what is *there*? Are there not also feelings and emotions associated with this object? Is not the extraordinary sound that the violin is capable of producing also evoked, and thus an integral part of this perception? When you enter an airport terminal and see that your beloved friend is walking towards you, is not this perceptual feat of face recognition also accompanied by emotion? And what about the emotions aroused as a direct result of the very *absence* of perceiving what we had expected and hoped for? The following is an illustration of this negating aspect, so to speak, of perception:

. . . I go into a café, expecting to see a friend, Pierre, and discover by perception, and immediately, that he is not there. The café and all the other people fall immediately into a background, against which I expect to see Pierre stand out. But he does not. . . . Of course, many other people besides Pierre are not in the café at any particular moment. But that they are not is something which I may think, rather than perceive. The absence of someone whom I had expected to see is a perceived absence, an actual experienced negation or nothingness . . . (Warnock, 1992, p. 95)

So, the above paragraphs help to identify two main objections to the way in which the study of perception in psychology has often relied upon reduced or impoverished visual environments, notably in the form of visual illusions. (1) It is the whole person who is involved in perceiving. Hence, the study of perception cannot really be carried out as if the visual system can be taken in isolation from this whole. (2) The illustration from Warnock highlights the fact that it is not just vision that is involved, but that thinking and conceptualisation also play a part. In the Warnock example, it is actually the very absence of the expected visual input that is central to the perceptual experience itself. Although, admittedly, some of the well-known visual illusions also draw attention to this issue. The Kanizsa triangle, Figure 6.1, is a good example of this.

Similar criticisms of experimental reductionism have been levelled against the study of memory where participants try to recall so-called nonsense syllables. When, in real life, would anyone be expected to use their memory in this fashion? Again, the counter-argument to this objection would, of course, be that it is only by simplifying the world that we can start to see how things really work.

The evolutionary perspective

Psychology is often defined as the study of human behaviour and experience. 'Experience' in this context does not, of course, mean the same thing as when we refer to someone having a great deal of life experience (in the sense, for example, that we might talk about an experienced teacher or therapist). Rather, here what is referred to is anything to do with the 'contents' of the 'mind': thinking; feelings, such as fear, jealousy, etc.; information processing; problem solving; memory; perception; and so on. In defining the term 'experience', some psychologists would also include dreams and the activities of the unconscious, whether the individual is asleep and dreaming or awake and not consciously aware of what is being thought about at a 'deep' level. Also included might be information processing which can take place without acknowledged awareness that it is going on. (This category might include studies of subliminal perception and the so-called 'blindsight' phenomenon investigated by Weiskrantz, 1986.)

When psychologists study human behaviour and experience, they are engaged in asking questions about why humans exhibit the behaviour that they do, and why it is that they have the kind of mental experiences that they do. These seem quite straightforward questions to pose. The problem lies in the fact that different kinds of answers to the 'why?' questions can be given. In fact the sort of answer given rather depends upon the level or point at which you decide to attribute causation. Consider the following 'why' question: Why did the mother put the hungry infant to her breast? Now, three very different kinds of answers to this question could be as follows.

(1) The behaviour in question can be seen in terms of its *causation*. What caused the mother to behave in this way was simply that the child was crying. Such an answer, of course, is simply stated in terms of a cause-and-effect relationship between the mother's behaviour – putting the infant to her breast – and what happened just prior to this – the baby crying. Psychologists would tend to refer to the child's crying as an *antecedent* to the behaviour of the mother.

(2) The behaviour in question can also be explained by antecedents over a much longer time scale. Here the explanation offered might be in terms of the mother's own personal development. So, to explain appropriate, 'good', mothering behaviour, as is the case here, you might need/wish to investigate what it is that makes a 'good' mother. What was it in this mother's lifelong development that thankfully has resulted in her being able to exhibit the appropriate response, that is, to produce behaviour which benefits the infant? Not all mothers develop in such a way that they exhibit the desired/appropriate mothering response. This particular aspect of development might, amongst other things, be traced to psychological factors. Such factors might include the kind of mothering the mother under observation was herself subjected to, and so on.

(3) The above answers to the question 'why' are provided in terms of immediate and longer-term causation. The immediate cause is perhaps quite straightforward. The longer-term causation is a little more difficult to tease out and problematic because this causation is proposed

over a longer period of time, and one which involves the now unseen history of the individual. However, neither of the above two answers is really sufficient to answer the very heart of the question posed.

Now, everybody knows that a crying baby will produce this response in a nurturing mother. We all know that the baby's cry usually means that it is hungry or in some kind of discomfort. However, this has still not answered the question as to why it is specifically the crying that elicits this response. This really has to do with addressing a question that goes way beyond the recent history of what the child has just done and what has happened to the mother during her life. In fact, it has more to do with how the species has developed. Here then, we must address the much longer-term history concerning how the human species has come to evolve in such a way that the crying and the feeding go together. We are concerned here with the evolutionary fact that behaviour is driven ultimately by genes. This is to say that the process of evolution involves a fine-tuning of the species whereby those individual members of the species who have the 'healthiest' genes will tend to survive. By healthiest what is meant is survival value in terms of adaptability to the environment, and inevitably this refers to the likelihood of successful reproduction, and hence survival of those particular genes. Put crudely, then, the argument would be as follows: the baby cries, and importantly, cries at the pitch, volume, intensity, persistence, etc. that it does, because only those individual members of the species who throughout the process of evolution exhibited the most effective behaviour for signalling hunger were fed, and hence stood a chance of surviving and probably going on to reproduce. Ineffective cries would thus die out. But why does the mother respond at all? It is easy to see the survival value for the infant but why should the mother respond to the cry?

At this point in the argument it is much more productive to avoid moralistic, emotional or sentimental answers to the question just posed. The mother responds because she too has a vested interest in the baby's survival. The baby that she has produced is carrying half of the mother's genes. The mother's behaviour is driven not by a desire to protect her own skin, rather it is driven by the genetic and evolutionary imperative or command to ensure the survival of her genes – nothing less, nothing more. A crying baby triggers the flow of milk in a lactating female. Again, it could be suggested that during the evolutionary process, females who didn't respond in this manner very effectively would prove to be inefficient feeders for the young. This inefficiency, itself genetically based, would thus die out because the baby would not be fed adequately, hence the mother's genes would not be passed on. So, if this evolutionary explanation can best be described as reductionist, and if such reductionism implies a more basic and more compelling explanation than other explanations, why is this so, and what happens to the other rather less reduced explanations for behaviour? What, then, is their status? The next section considers these questions.

Consequences for psychology

Going back to the question posed previously, what exactly is meant by suggesting that we should avoid moralistic, emotional or sentimental answers? Well, it's just that evolutionary-grounded arguments only concentrate on the idea that successful behaviours ensure survival of the animal, reproduction and furtherance of the animal's genes. Any behaviours that fail to serve these purposes will logically become extinct. Now the logical conclusion must be that the mother feeds the hungry infant by putting it to her breast because she is genetically programmed to do so. Thus, the explanation is very simple and straightforward. As such, it is not necessary to call upon everyday explanations because such explanations are over-elaborate translations of this very simple genetically-driven behaviour. A *moralistic* explanation of the mother's behaviour would state that the mother fed the hungry child because that is what a good mother's sense of duty will tell her that she ought to do. Similarly, *emotional* explanations will talk about the bond of love that ties a mother to her infant. Adopting the *sentimental* attitude will result in a conversation about how we feel so sorry for this beautiful, innocent, helpless little being.

Now, all of this does not in any way imply that moral attitudes and emotional sentiments do not exist. Nor does it suggest that they are of no importance in the study of humans. What it does suggest is that what may appear to be quite complex is actually driven by genetic programming. Any talk about love, duty, pity, etc., is purely a by-product of the fact that we have consciousness. Organisms that do not have consciousness go about the business of caring for their young quite dutifully but without ever knowing what duty is. Like the human mother, they are only ensuring the survival of the young, and importantly, the survival of their genes.

Review exercise

Re-read the section above concerning the evolutionary perspective. With its arguments in mind, consider the following case:

Kevin is studying for his degree in psychology. His ambition is eventually to become an educational psychologist, which is quite a well-paid career. He has been married to Jan for just one year, and they are expecting their first child. Kevin is working very hard and Jan has been extremely supportive.

Write down answers to the following questions:

(1) *In terms of the evolutionary perspective*, why is Kevin making this effort?
(2) *In terms of the evolutionary perspective*, why is Jan being so supportive?
(3) Why can this evolutionary perspective be described as reductionist?

Summary

The concluding section above concerning the evolutionary perspective is a good example of the very problem surrounding reductionist accounts in psychology. Obviously psychologists must concern themselves with attempting to discover the truth concerning what really drives behaviour. Indeed, there appears to be something quite persuasive and 'true' about the evolutionary perspective. It would be difficult in fact to argue against the idea that our behaviour is genetically driven. Of course the mother in the example provided above is 'programmed' to respond to the cries of the hungry infant. The problem is, however, that we *do* have consciousness. And, although the mother's feelings of love for her child seem to be dismissed above as merely a by-product of consciousness, this is a very important by-product. The point is this: are not feelings such as love, pity, a sense of duty, anger, despair, etc. really the very things that make us human? And is not the study of human beings, and everything that goes with being human, the very aim of psychology?

Reductionist accounts, then, do just what the word suggests: they reduce whatever is being explained down to its component parts, and this act of reduction brings with it the danger that important 'realities' somehow disappear. A simple comparison should help to illustrate this point: if you wanted to provide a reductionist account of the chair you are sitting in, or of the very pages that you are at present reading, you could do so by accounting for these objects in terms of the atoms of matter of which they are composed. But an account which talks about atoms is no longer talking about the 'higher' level, the *idea* of a chair or a book.

The next chapter provides a detailed example of some of the problems associated with reductionist accounts of the mind–body problem.

Further reading

Jarvis, M. (2000) *Theoretical Approaches in Psychology*, London: Routledge. Chapters 8 and 9 provide a clear account of genetic and biological influences on behaviour. From the same series as *Debates in Psychology*.

Ridley, M. (1994) *The Red Queen*, London: Penguin Books. A comprehensive account of the influence of genetic factors upon behaviour.

4

Reductionism and the mind–body problem

- What is the mind–body problem?
- Various positions on the mind–body problem
- Reasons why there is a mind–body problem
- Summary

What is the mind–body problem?

This chapter provides an in-depth illustration of the way in which reductionism applies to a fundamental issue in psychology. Explained here are the various positions that psychologists and philosophers hold concerning the possible relationships which might exist between mind and body. Some reasons as to why this problem still persists are suggested. The main arguments for and against a reductionist view of the mind are presented. In this context, of course, reductionism implies that *all* thoughts, sensations, ideas, feelings, decisions and emotions will ultimately be explained in terms of physical processes. That is to say that all of psychology can, at least in principle, be reduced to biology and physics. It will be suggested that what we call the mind is merely a vaguely defined word in our vocabulary, and it remains this way for three main reasons:

(a) The idea of 'mind' remains simply because of the misleading manner in which we talk about things.

(b) The word 'mind' is often only used when we need to fill in any gaps in our current knowledge about what goes on at the biological level. In principle, we may one day have a complete understanding of the underlying physiological factors. When we have that knowledge, there will be no gaps, and hence there will be no need to invent the mind.

(c) Some views or positions concerning the concept of mind assert that mind exists at a metaphysical level. This simply means that it stands somehow apart from or above the physical world. If it is really true that mind is not a physical 'thing', then it takes on something of a ghostly nature because it cannot logically be studied in the same manner as the physical world.

First, it is important to remember that when the mind–body problem is discussed, the word body includes the brain. So when discussing this issue, psychologists and philosophers will sometimes refer to the mind–body problem, but sometimes they will use the expression: the mind–brain problem.

Various positions on the mind–body problem

Dualism

The principal dualist position is one that asserts that the mind is not physical. Most dualist positions regard mind and body as being causally related. This, of course, presents a particular philosophical problem. The brain being physical in nature is necessarily located in a particular place. However, the *mind* is a non-physical, metaphysical concept. It is therefore non-spatial and non-physical by definition. How then can they influence each other? How can mind prod matter into action, or vice versa? Furthermore, if they interact causally, then where in the world would this take place? How could they possibly affect each other given that metaphysical entities are actually not of this world. Two types of dualism, interactionism and epiphenomenalism, are discussed next.

(a) Interactionism

This position holds that the causal relationship between mind and body works in both directions: the mind can influence the body, and the body can influence the mind.

Physical →
    ← Mental

In everyday speech we talk about the mind and the body. In fact, many statements about mind imply some kind of connection with the body and vice versa. For example, LSD is referred to as a mind-altering drug. This implies that the physical presence of this drug in the body causes changes in a person's mind. By altering the physical circumstances within the body, the result is a change in the way in which the mind functions. Similarly, humans, and indeed 'lower' animals, with damage to the corpus callosum – the area of the brain that connects the two hemispheres – often appear to be 'in two minds' (Sperry, 1961 and 1984). They appear to be in two minds because both halves of the brain seem to act independently of each other when such damage has occurred. Also, electrical stimulation of specific parts of the cerebral cortex causes particular 'mind events' such as sensations and memories (Penfield and Rasmussen, 1950).

In everyday language there would appear to be numerous assertions that this causal relationship is two-way rather than just one-way. We often talk in a manner implying that the mind can somehow cause physical events in a person's body. Thus, a person can be said to have finally *made up their mind* about something, and it is exactly this that causes the person to perform a particular physical action. For example, to make another cup of coffee; to call 'heads' rather than 'tails' at the toss of a coin; to drive to work rather than take the bus; finally to start writing an essay, and so on. There are numerous other examples which imply the effects of mind upon matter. In fact, we actually talk about mind over matter. This means, for example, that the right state of mind can have a real effect upon the body. Talking about a patient's determination to beat an illness such as cancer is an example. There are accounts of mothers who, due to their desperate state of mind, find the energy and the physical capability to lift a car to free a trapped child. Psychosomatic illnesses imply that it is a state of mind that causes very real and apparent physical health problems. Football managers will urge their players to have the right mental attitude necessary to perform well during a match.

The main idea here is that there are two distinct things, mind and body, and these have an effect upon each other in the ways just described. However, just exactly how a physical body can interact with a metaphysical entity, the mind, and vice versa, remains a real problem with respect to this position on the mind–body issue.

(b) Epiphenomenalism

The above examples all assert that body and mind are causally related. Epiphenomenalism asserts that what we call mind is reducible *in origin* to physical matter, at least in the sense that mind is the one-way product of physical events in the brain. The causal relationship works here only in one direction.

$$Physical \rightarrow Mental$$

An epiphenomenon can be defined as a secondary phenomenon accompanying another and directly caused by it. Thus, to take an epiphenomenalist position on the mind–body issue is to assert that what we call the mind is something that is somehow separate from the brain but produced by it. Mind is a phenomenon which exists in addition to or accompanying the physical processes of the brain. Mind is caused by these processes.

According to an epiphenomenalist, mental experiences or processes are seen as non-causal by-products of physical processes. Here only physical processes are regarded as having causal powers. This position is rather different to the way in which we talk about the relationship between mind and body in everyday conversation. Several of the examples above certainly do reflect our common-sense belief that mind can causally affect the body. Epiphenomenalism can be viewed as a type of reductionism in that although we still have two distinct things – physical and mental events – the *origin* of mental states is seen as being causally located in the physical. The mind isn't already there, so to speak, as a separate entity. It is produced by the body, or, more precisely, the brain. No separate, mysterious life-giving mind, spirit or life-force needs to be called upon to explain how thoughts come into existence. They are simply products of the physical processes of the brain. Just as digestion is achieved in and through the stomach, then, similarly, mental events are achieved in and through the brain. Indeed, John Searle asks a very interesting question about this:

> Why do we still have in philosophy and psychology after all these centuries a 'mind–body problem' in a way that we do not have,

say, a 'digestion–stomach problem'? Why does the mind seem more mysterious than other biological phenomena? (Searle, 1991, p. 14)

Monism

Dualist positions, by definition, mean that two things exist: mind and body. And if it is true that these two distinct and causally related things exist, the problem centres around examining the way in which they are causally related. Monist positions on the mind–body issue can be regarded as particularly reductionist because they propose that this very examination of the causal relationship between mind and body is actually an unnecessarily over-complex debate to even get into in the first place. Monist positions, then, assert that only one thing actually exists. Needless to say, these positions propose that either only the mind exists or only the physical processes of the body exist. These two positions are known as (a) idealism and (b) materialism respectively.

(a) Idealism

Idealism is regarded as reductionist because it asserts that one thing only exists: the mind. It suggests that only mental phenomena exist. The entire universe is purely and only inhabited by mind. It must be stated from the very start here that this position is not particularly popular amongst psychologists or philosophers. It does, however, present some thought-provoking ideas.

The philosopher Kant proposed a well-known riddle. It asked: 'If a tree falls in the forest and nobody is there to hear it falling, does it still make a noise as it falls?'

If you think about this question properly, it is not quite as silly as it sounds. The first common-sense reaction is to say: 'Of course it makes a noise. It's just that nobody is there to hear it doing so.' But what does the expression 'to make a noise' actually mean? When we say that something makes a noise, this inevitably implies that we mean that it makes a noise as someone perceives it. If the tree 'wants' to make a noise, so to speak, it depends upon someone actually being there to hear it falling. Assuming that the tree itself doesn't have the power of hearing then, in the absence of somebody being there to hear, where would this 'thing' called noise actually exist?

Now, the idealist position asserts that the only direct knowledge or acquaintance that we have of anything in the world is our own minds. This is an undeniable fact because any knowledge that we have of absolutely anything else in the world is indirect knowledge. The above riddle really concerns the question of what the world is really like.

Again, the natural response to the last sentence might be to say: 'Of course I know what the world is really like. I experience the world through my five senses, do I not? And how I experience it is how it is.' But is it necessarily true to claim this? Kant would assert that this 'world' that we know is not really there. Not as we know it at least. This world is never directly known, rather it is 'filtered through our senses'. Coming back to Kant's riddle then, if there was no such thing as the sense of hearing, then nothing could ever be heard. Hence logically nothing could ever make a noise without the sense of hearing. So, of course the tree wouldn't make any noise if nobody was there to hear it.

Idealism, then, proposes that only mental phenomena are real and knowable. If the world contains anything other than mental 'reality', then where is the rest of this world? And what is it really like? With idealism, then, the only thing that we know to really exist is the mind.

Kant's ideas concerning phenomenology have important implications for any claims that science can be objective. Phenomenology suggests that if sense data are limited or flawed in terms of 'getting at' the 'real world', then science itself must logically be similarly fallible because science itself relies upon interpretation of sense data.

(b) Materialism

Sometimes also referred to as *physicalism*, this stance, as the name suggests, asserts the very opposite of idealism. But here again, two things are reduced to just one. Here there is no problem concerning how mind and body interact. For here, mind is seen as being reducible to physical processes. Here mental events *are* physical events. Or to put it another way, we have only come to talk about mental events in the first place because we are deluded into believing that they exist as separate entities from the physical processes of the brain. Reductionist stances inevitably propose that what is being looked at is actually something less complex than has traditionally been taken as the case.

In the case of the dualist perspective proposed by interactionism it could be claimed that this led to an inevitably over-complicated discussion concerning how and where mind and body exert causal influence over each other. The materialist stance would claim that this is over-complicated simply because the very concept of mind is itself delusory: the word mind is nothing but a linguistic artefact or creation. In other words, mind is a construct rather than a reality.

Psychiatry, itself being medically based, has traditionally tended to be materialist in its approach. Thus, for example, the project of assisting people with the disturbed and disturbing states of mind associated with schizophrenia has involved the use of drugs such as tranquillisers. Similarly manic depression, or bi-polar disorder, as it is referred to nowadays, has typically been treated by adjustments of the lithium level in the patient's body. The logic here is simply that by influencing physical processes with this kind of physical intervention what is achieved is an alteration of the patient's state of mind.

Sperry's article (1984) is reviewed in Chapter Eight, and it examines the effects and implications of surgically separating the two hemispheres of the brain, and effectively dividing the brain into apparently independently functioning halves. (This operation is performed in order to control severe epilepsy.) If, as the materialist position would insist, mind equals brain processes, does this now mean that such 'split-brain' patients now possess two independent minds? Indeed, the research detailed in Sperry's article would suggest that such patients do in fact behave as if they were literally 'in two minds'. Or, as the materialist would have it, two separate 'people' inhabiting 'two brains'.

What are the implications of materialism? Getting the thoughts to think for themselves

Bottom-up and top-down causation were discussed in the examination of free will in Chapter Two. Of importance is the idea that when we talk about deciding to do anything it feels as though there is a separate thing that does the willing. Thus, I might decide to raise my right arm, to read a book, etc., and the point is that it might feel as though there is something that we often call the mind that 'hovers around' and 'makes its mind up' to do any of these things. But this is illusory, and it is illusory simply because any decision that we make, any thought that we have, is itself a physical process. Invoking the metaphysical concept of mind unnecessarily over-complicates matters: 'Are we supposed to think that our thoughts and feelings can somehow produce chemical effects on our brains and the rest of the nervous system? How could such a thing occur? Are we supposed to think that thoughts can wrap themselves around the axons or shake the dendrites or sneak inside the cell wall and attack the cell nucleus?' (Searle, 1991, p. 17).

Reductionism in principle and in practice

Behaviourism tended to dissolve rather than resolve the mind–body problem. For the behaviourist, mind was ignored because it didn't lend itself to public observation. The issue was shelved rather than properly tackled. On the other hand, materialism approaches the problem head-on and asserts that mind is at best a social word that we use to talk about how it feels to *be* this human body, how it feels to be *in* – or rather simply to *be* – this body which has these physical processes. Some of these physical processes are processes in and of the brain. If materialism is true when it comes to what we call the mind, then an obvious answer to the traditional question of whether in principle a machine could have a mind, or whether a machine could think, is a resounding 'yes'. It could be argued that machines do indeed already think. What else is a chess-playing machine doing when it plays a good game of chess? Furthermore, as we know, chess-playing machines do play extremely good games of chess. Materialism reduces mental events down to physical processes. Thus, in principle, it only becomes a matter of creating a functional equivalent in machine form to the physical processes of the brain. The only major difference between the machine and the brain is that the latter is made out of organic matter and the former of inorganic. Thus thinking loses its mystical quality. 'Thinking' *is* a series of physical processes, no more, no less. As with the word 'thinking', the word 'belief' can also be seen as nothing more mystical than these physical processes:

> ... McCarthy, the inventor of the term 'artificial intelligence' ... says even 'machines as simple as thermostats can be said to have beliefs ... my thermostat has three beliefs – it is too hot in here, it is too cold in here, and it is just right in here.' (Searle, 1991, p. 30)

As with the word thinking, it very much depends upon your definition of the word belief. If I believe that it is raining because I can hear a particular sound against the window, then what is meant by belief here is that there is some particular representation in my head with reference to something out there in the world. Whether or not this belief is true is another matter. It might not actually be raining at all. The noise could be due to something else hitting the window. Having a belief is a mental event, and mental events are physical processes which are about something other than the processes themselves. This 'aboutness' is referred to by philosophers as **intentionality**. McCarthy's thermostat similarly has this 'aboutness'. Indeed, a properly functioning thermostat will go through particular physical processes in terms of how they relate to events outside of these processes. A thermostat that works properly could therefore be said to have particular and correct beliefs about the world outside.

What do two people have in common when they both believe it is raining outside?

The section above attempts to examine mental events as processes. In particular the central idea is that mental processes such as thinking and having beliefs can in principle be replicated in machines because, after all, all of these imply some kind of physical process. Nothing as mysterious as mind needs to be introduced.

In practice, however, the main problem surrounding the reductionist project when it comes to brain processes is that the same mental process could be achieved in various, different structures. In other words, functional equivalents can be achieved through a variety of physical connections between neurones in the brain, etc. Such connections could vary from one person to another, or indeed could vary for any individual at different points in time. Or, to put it another way: if you and I both believe that it is raining outside, what have we got in common in terms of the physical processes and structures that exist in our heads? What is going on in my head may be quite different from what is going on in yours, although our belief about whether or not it is raining may be the same.

Reasons why there is a mind–body problem

A result of the confusing status of mind in clinical psychology

It is easy to see why the argument concerning the existence of mind has flourished in the clinical domain. It is very easy to talk about mental illness, but consider what this really implies. If the mind is a separate non-physical entity, then how can it be ill in the same way that the body can be ill? Talking about the mind being 'ill' is surely a kind of category error. Unless the mind really is reducible to body, a brain only, then this sort of labelling makes little sense. The mind is being discussed as if it could belong to a particular category of things that can become sick. And, unless you are deliberately talking in a metaphorical (or comparative) manner, illness and sickness are what can happen to biological entities, not to non-physical entities such as the mind. The reason that this sickness model was first proposed by those caring for people with psychological problems, is that it was the result of what might be referred to as a 'tactical error'.

Tactical error and mental illness

This idea of a tactical error suggests that psychiatrists didn't necessarily really believe that all psychological problems were the result of physical illness. In other words, they didn't particularly (or necessarily) believe in the physical reductionism of mental states. What they did believe in was that they should employ political tactics to ensure the best possible treatment for those with emotional and psychological disturbances. So, a deliberate comparison with physical illness was made in order to make sure that the insane received humane care. In other words, that they were given treatment comparable to that which was given to patients with evident physical illness and disease. Cochrane (1983) explains the historical rationale of this essentially reductionist approach in psychiatry:

> The use of the 'sickness' analogy, or more generally the medicalization of psychological and behavioural problems . . . arose for a number of reasons, all of them understandable in a historical context. First, there was the undoubted success that was being achieved by physical medicine in dealing with the

problems with which it was confronted: those dealing with psychological problems perhaps wanted to achieve the status and effectiveness of medical practitioners. Secondly there was the discovery that certain mental conditions did in fact have a physical basis – notably that general paralysis of the insane (GPI) was the result of an earlier infection with syphilis. This led to an assumption, which is still widespread, that all mental illness would be traced to an underlying biological cause. Third, there was the undoubted desire on the part of many psychiatrists to improve the treatment of the insane . . . by gaining something of the special status and tolerance reserved for the physically ill for those with psychological problems. (pp. 145–146)

A result of the way in which we talk about things

The mind–body problem and everyday speech

Many academics in psychology departments in British universities and elsewhere in the world are interested not so much in doing experiments in controlled laboratory set-ups, and therefore producing data of a quantitative nature, but rather in examining more qualitative material in the form of text and speech. There has been a move towards taking as data per se the things that people actually say, and write, either in everyday contexts or in more formal interview set-ups with the investigating psychologist. Examining documents written during different historical periods can also provide useful indications as to how people have tended to feel and think about things at different points in time. The following is an example of how the idea of 'mind' has been talked and written about.

In Shakespeare's play, Hamlet writes a letter to his girlfriend Ophelia. At the end of this letter he concludes with his promise of everlasting love. He writes, 'Adieu. Thine evermore, most dear lady, whilst this machine is to him, Hamlet.'

This example in particular is revealing in terms of the way in which it might be claimed that it discloses culturally-held attitudes and beliefs at the time that Shakespeare was writing. Simply examining the way that people talk about things can be extremely informative. In concluding his letter in this manner to his girlfriend, Hamlet could be said to be adopting what is referred to as a dualist stance regarding the mind–body issue. Examine closely exactly what he writes. First, it is revealing that he talks about his body as a mechanical entity, a machine. But, what or who is the 'him' that possesses this 'machine'? Is there some kind of ghost inhabiting the machine? Is there a duality suggested here? That is, two separate things: the machine – that is, the body – and the person, mind or soul that inhabits this body? The body is talked about here as if it were a temporary biological residence inhabited by something else.

Does something necessarily exist just because it's in our vocabulary?

Progress exercise

Compose a list of sentences which contain the word 'mind'. Analyse each of your sentences and decide what each implies with respect to the mind–body problem. For example, consider the following sentence: The patient was evidently completely out of his mind. The language used here suggests that this patient's body had become separated from his rightful mind. The patient might be seen to be possessed by another less healthy mind.

The rather ghostly concept of mind and soul is still used within the vocabulary of most languages. For example, consider the following German expression: Er hat einen regen Geist. This means in English: He has a good (or incisive/well-functioning) mind. But note that the word for mind here, Geist, literally translates as 'ghost' or 'spirit'. It is not difficult, then, to see how in language we talk about things as if they really exist. But, do things really exist just because we talk about them? After all, we can talk about tables, chairs, Los Angeles, and the Alps. But we can also talk about the Abominable Snowman and about fairies living at the bottom of the garden. When we use the word 'goodbye', what we are actually saying is a shortened or contracted version of 'God be with you'. Thus, when we say this as someone leaves our company, we are certainly wishing them well. And when we take leave of someone that we know we are never going to see again, when the other person is dying for example, we use the word 'Adieu'. A word which literally means 'until God'. In other words: 'until we both stand before God after death'. The point here is, of course, that language can and does survive outdated ways of thinking. Whether or not you personally believe in God, the word survives in the language employed by non-believers and believers alike. Even the most ardent atheist amongst us uses the term 'goodbye' when parting from a friend, or thinks and talks about a musician's or a writer's 'God-given skills'. Similarly, the French equivalent of our expression 'to have nine lives' is literally translated as 'to have your soul rawl-plugged onto your body'. Both expressions are used when talking about someone who has had many narrow escapes from life-threatening situations. The French expression is particularly quaint and perhaps amusing, and again is used by many French people who don't necessarily believe that the body is really inhabited by a soul or mind.

The mind–body problem and artificial intelligence

It is interesting, then, to see the mechanistic manner in which the body is being viewed in the earlier quotation from *Hamlet*. However, this is not really much different from the way that many psychologists working within artificial intelligence today claim that thinking could be replicated in a machine. This is a claim which often has at its root the belief that this is possible in principle because human beings are nothing more than complex machines which just happen to produce thought. This last statement might be taken as an example of a particular stance (discussed earlier in this chapter) concerning the mind–body issue called epiphenomenalism. This refers to a belief that mental states are very real, although non-physical, by-products of the brain.

The idea of mind in everyday language

With regard to the way that we talk everyday, what clues are offered concerning the idea that the mind–body problem still exists? Or at least that we think and talk about two different but somehow related things: mind and body. How do we talk about people who have died? We do not talk about taking Mr Smith down to the mortuary. It is Mr Smith's *body* that is taken. Talking in this manner suggests that the Mr Smith who owned the body is now separated from it. We might refer to a friend as having an attractive body or as having a good physique. How odd it would be to say to someone that you think they are an attractive body. Saying this would probably prove to be an extremely ineffective chat-up line at a night-club, for it would imply an impolite and insultingly reductionist view of the other person, as if they were nothing but a body rather than a body inhabited by a person, soul, spirit, etc. Furthermore, people don't want to be admired and loved just for their body, but who or what might it be that possesses or inhabits this body? It is perhaps at this point that we find ourselves forced to call upon words like person, soul, spirit, mind. We might say that someone is attractive, but that would be different for it suggests that this is only one of the adjectives that you could use to describe the whole person that inhabits the body. We might apply other adjectives to the same person such as generous, kind, good. That is to say that we might use adjectives which describe the whole person or personality. This, of course, is the central issue surrounding the mind–body problem: whereas the body is physical and hence accessible to scientific or objective investigation, the mind is metaphysical in nature, illusive, hidden and subjectively experienced. This subjectivity, of course, is one of the main factors that make the concept of 'mind' so problematic.

Having knowledge of the mind: your own and the minds of others

The body is a physical thing. It is publicly available, so to speak. It can be touched, walked around, measured, and indeed talked about. However, when it comes to the mind, we can only really talk about it. Reducing the mind to a specific physical location is the real practical problem. Whereas all bodies are publicly available to everyone, when it comes to the mind there is only the private access of the individual mind to itself. I have access to my mind, thoughts, etc. in a way that only I can have. I can never have direct access to the mind of another person. This is referred to as the 'problem of other minds'. An appreciation of this issue concerning the very private nature of mind is fundamental to approaching an understanding of exactly why the mind–body problem would seem to be an intractable (or obstinate) difficulty in psychological study.

Only I can know my own thoughts directly. I can infer what you might be thinking by your behaviour, but I can never ever have access to your thoughts in the way that you do. Similarly, I can know, indirectly, that you are in pain by your screams, etc., but I can never know your pain in the very real and immediate manner that you can. Nor could you ever know mine:

> What about the part of mental life which a man can see? It is a difficult question, no matter what one's point of view, partly because it raises the question of what seeing means and partly because the events seen are private. The fact of privacy cannot, of course, be questioned. Each person is in special contact with a small part of the universe enclosed within his own skin. . . . Though two people may in some sense be said to see the same light or hear the same sound, they cannot feel the same distention of a bile duct or the same bruised muscle. (When privacy is invaded with scientific instruments, the form of stimulation is changed; the scales read by the scientists are not the private events themselves.) (Skinner, in Wann, 1964, p. 82)

The impossibility of gaining objective access to the mind

So inner experiences and events are by definition private. Even attempting to 'invade' these events only 'gets at' the physiological events associated with the particular private experiences, not the experience itself. At the end of the above quotation, Skinner makes the point that the very act of trying to observe what is going on in the brain actually changes the very thing that is being observed. This last point is a very important philosophical issue applicable to any scientific endeavour. Whether in physics, biology, psychology, or whatever discipline, the observer is always a part of that which is being observed. In this sense, true objectivity is always an ideal, rather than an achievable goal for the scientist. Put simply, if a thermometer is used to measure the temperature of water, the temperature of the thermometer itself will, however much or little, either cool down or warm up the water itself. Along the same lines, investigators in psychology must always be aware that the very presence of the experimenter is likely to change or affect the behaviour of the participants under investigation. So, even if it were technically possible to get into another person's experiences or thoughts, the investigator would only get there at one remove, so to speak: the experiences and thoughts would be changed by the very act of being observed.

Biopsychologists, however, do study the brain, and they have a variety of methods at their disposal for doing so. For example, EEG (electroencephalogram) is used to record the activity of a large number of neurones from outside the skull. This has been used largely for studying brain-state correlates in states of awareness and stages of sleep. Microelectrodes can record the activity of individual neurones. For instance, Hubel and Wiesel (1959) were particularly successful at building up a 'map' of the hierarchical arrangement of the visual system in cats and monkeys by employing this technique. (They discovered that there were what they labelled 'simple', 'complex' and 'hyper-complex' cells in the visual system which would fire discriminately in the presence of particular visual stimuli of varying degrees of complexity.) The point here is, however, that the investigators only observed the physical neuronal events *associated* with the organism's visual experience. The experience itself remains private and directly unknowable to anyone except the organism actually having the experience. Hence the investigator would never be able to observe the cat's or monkey's very private *experience* of seeing.

Review exercise

By re-reading/referring back to the relevant sub-sections in this chapter, consider each of the following 'positions' regarding the mind–body question:

(1) Interactionism
(2) Epiphenomenalism
(3) Idealism
(4) Materialism

Now, having reviewed each of these positions, write brief notes concerning:

(a) which position you personally most agree with, and why you agree with it;
(b) which position you least agree with, and why;
(c) which position, or positions, are most strongly in line with religious or spiritual concerns regarding the soul, the after-life, etc.;
(d) how you personally feel about what you now believe concerning the mind–body question.

Summary

The major positions concerning the mind–body issue have been outlined in this chapter. In terms of the debate concerning reductionism in psychology, the material presented here could be drawn upon for examples of the problems that arise when we attempt to explain 'mind' in terms of physical processes. In this chapter it was noted that those who hold the materialist position believe that what we call 'mental events' are in fact physical processes in the brain. For the materialist, there is only physical matter to talk about. The problem is, of course, that this line of argument tends to dissolve rather than resolve the mind–body issue for many psychologists. When we talk about the mind, we are talking about a 'reality' which all of us experience in a very private way. For most people the idea of 'mind' is not at all an idea about something physical in the first place. Thus, to suggest that 'mind' can be reduced to something merely physical is to make a basic error from the very start.

Further reading

Searle, J. (1984) *Minds, Brains & Science*, London: Penguin. Chapter 1: 'The mind–body problem'.

Nagel, T. (1987) *What Does It All Mean? A Very Short Introduction to Philosophy*, Oxford: Oxford University Press. Chapter 4: 'The mind–body problem'.

Hospers, J. (1990) *An Introduction to Philosophical Analysis*, 3rd edn, London: Routledge. Chapter 6: 'Mind and body'.

5

Can psychology be a science?

What exactly is science?

Science . . . a branch of systematized knowledge . . . something (e.g. a skill or technique) that may be studied or learned systematically . . . the possession of knowledge . . . as opposed to ignorance or misunderstanding.

(*Longman Dictionary of the English Language*, 1984)

Psychologists' attempts to create systematised knowledge inevitably concern efforts to discover consistencies and generalities about human behaviour and experience. This involves statements which include the words, *if . . . then*.

For example, *if* a physically attractive person is interviewed for a job, *then* that person is generally perceived as having more positive qualities than a less attractive candidate, this being known as the 'halo effect'. *If* a patient is suffering from bi-polar disorder (manic depression) *then* it is generally found that the patient has an abnormal level of lithium in the blood. *If* a rat is rewarded with food for pressing a bar and is only rewarded at variable intervals, *then* the behaviour will be more resistant to **extinction** than when it had been rewarded continuously, i.e. each time the bar is pressed. *If* a person suffers a stroke and loses language abilities, *then* it is generally the case that the stroke occurred in the left hemisphere of the cerebral cortex.

In other words, the kind of knowledge that is gathered through science is concerned with looking for and discovering generalities. Gaining this kind of information about such regularities helps us to understand how the world works. It also helps us to predict and to control. Notice that the next logical argument contains two *if . . . then* statements: *If* we notice that (*if*) whenever we come into close contact with someone with a cold, (*then*) we ourselves tend to become ill, *then* in future we are likely to try to avoid coming into close contact with people with colds.

Thus, it could be said by looking at the above example that, in a way, all people are scientists of a sort. Just living our lives involves us in looking for regularities and patterns in order to predict what is likely to happen next. Thinking and observing in this *If . . . then* manner is not confined to scientists working within academic disciplines. Insurance companies look at the overall pattern when deciding how much to charge a particular driver for an insurance policy. A young man with two years' driving experience (the '*if*') is generally more likely to get involved in an accident than a middle-aged woman with many years of experience (the '*then*'). Of course there are exceptions. However, as with the scientist, what is of interest is the generality, not the relatively rare and comparatively unique case.

Thus scientists strive to seek out regularities. The pure sciences have not only uncovered regularities but laws of nature. In other words they have uncovered invariants. Thus, light obeys the law of refraction. That is, it always and invariably bends to a predictable degree as it passes from one medium to another. Water always boils at sea level at 212° F, and so on.

Overview of points raised on 'scientific' approaches to psychology

To some extent the question as to whether or not psychology can or should be a science is inevitably touched upon in several other chapters in this text. When examining behaviourism (Chapter Seven) several points are made with reference to the idea of psychology's attempts to align itself with the 'pure' sciences, to place itself alongside of the already extremely successful disciplines of physics, biology and chemistry. The word 'science' itself is directly derived from the Latin word meaning 'to know', 'scire'. When we talk about adopting scientific methods, for example, what we really mean is that we are adopting methods of knowing things about the world. However, it is not just a question of knowing things about the world. It is important to stress here that it is a question of knowing that what is known is actually true. This type of examination concerning the truth-value or status of knowledge is a branch of philosophy known as epistemology. Behaviourists, of course, insisted that the only knowledge which could seriously make a claim to having undeniable truth status is knowledge obtained through direct objective observation, rather than, for example, through speculation or through introspection. The behaviourist concentrates exclusively upon readily observable behaviour. It is important to underline that such behaviour needs to be readily observable, at least potentially, by more than one observer at the same time; thus, the subject matter of psychology was redefined. No longer should the definition of psychology, as it had in its early days, include the private domain of mind, thinking, etc. The publicly observable domain of behaviour was proposed as the proper subject matter for psychology.

This redefinition of psychology as an academic discipline inevitably involved the creation of a whole new vocabulary. Banished was mentalistic discourse (ways of talking) which included words such as 'thinking', 'motivation', 'sadness', 'indecision', etc. These were replaced by the rather more cold and mechanistic terminology which talked about 'schedules of reinforcement', 'extinction', 'antecedents of behaviour', 'negative reinforcement', etc. It was via these concepts that behaviourism promised, at last, to provide a **paradigm** for psychology. A paradigm, in science, means an agreed way of investigating and formulating knowledge about the world. The stated project of behaviourism was, therefore, to explain all behaviour within the framework of **associative**

learning. This approach, then, could indeed be described as scientific because there was something very certain about the data that it yielded to the investigator. For example, there was something certain about the way in which different schedules of reinforcement could be observed to have particular effects upon behaviour. In other words, here was a way of going about the business of 'doing' psychology which provided knowledge that was actually 'true'.

Problems associated with behaviourism: the price to be paid

The problem with this approach, of course, was that this redefinition of the scope of psychology no longer included the 'inner world' of the human mind. Scientific exactitude could only be achieved at the expense of dissolving, rather than solving, problems associated with the mind. In fact, the mechanical scientific precision associated with the essentially reductionist approach of extreme behaviourists, such as Skinner, might be compared to the same sort of destructive precision inherent in taking anything to pieces in order to see how it works. Little children, for example, wanting to discover and understand just how a mechanical toy works might take the toy to pieces. Although the pieces are now readily observable and in full view, there's no toy left to understand. Similarly, the behaviourist's endeavour to understand humans by reducing them to units of conditioned associations, albeit in complex arrangements, inevitably would leave the psychologist with no person to understand, only a collection of parts. This reduction of the individual to a number of parts is often referred to as 'reification'. This term is derived from the Latin word 'res' which means 'things'. This tendency to turn the person into an object or to view the individual as a thing is tied in with psychology's efforts to insist that human beings can – and indeed should – be studied in the same detached and objective manner that the pure sciences study the rest of the natural world. This objectification by definition de-personalises the individual. This has serious implications for psychology.

A truly scientific approach is one which clearly identifies universal cause-and-effect relationships. It is one which establishes the 'mechanics' of just exactly how things work. Behaviourism, of course, promised to provide just such an account. The real objection to behaviourism, however, was that in order to achieve this mechanistic version of human psychology, it had been necessary not only to eliminate mentalistic realities but also to go a long way down the phylogenetic scale by studying lower animals such as rats and pigeons. Much was learned about these animals and much was speculated as to how the principles that were thus teased out actually related to humans.

Causation

Free will and determinism (Chapter Two) inevitably involved an examination of causation. Science, of course, is mainly concerned with establishing a picture of how the world works by examining what causes what to happen and under what circumstances. Amongst many other impressive achievements, the 'pure' sciences were responsible for landing a man on the moon. Now that could only have been achieved by first arriving at a comprehensive knowledge concerning causation. Only by understanding causal relationships can the scientist manage to predict and control the world, and scientists needed to be able to predict and control an enormous number of things in order to get a man to the moon and back. How else would this be achieved? Free will, it was suggested, was an illusion, because if everything has a cause, then all behaviour – and all our thoughts – must be caused by something. Therefore, there is no such thing as real freedom. When viewed in this way the real aim of psychology (as a science) must be to discover exactly what is causing what. It can only be seen as a waste of time and a fundamental error to call upon arguments that suggest that it is the mind or an individual's free will that does the willing. It is no accident that when we make a prediction about our own future behaviour we use the very same word, will. Thus you might state: 'Tonight I will write an essay on the mind–body issue.' But this will has no powers of causation. Sadly, as we all know, stating your intentions and actually doing what has been stated can be two very different things. No statement about the future actually causes future events to happen. No statement concerning tomorrow, or indeed any point in the future, can be said to be true or to have predictive status. At the very best, you can wait until tomorrow has gone to see whether your prediction was actually true. Chapter Two posed the question concerning what it might be that actually does the willing. It was suggested that there is no separate non-physical ghostly 'thing' called the will or the mind that somehow has powers to cause anything to happen. If you think about it, this viewpoint insists that all causation is based ultimately within the physical world, so the argument that psychology should use the very same objective methods as the 'pure' sciences goes something like this: If everything is caused by something else, then all psychological states and all behaviour are caused. If all thoughts, ideas, intentions, feelings, projects, behaviour, emotions, etc. have a very real physical basis, then they don't just mysteriously come from nowhere. Hence, because they exist within the physical realm of the natural world just like everything else, it must be logical to propose that psychology can and should be studied in just the same objective and scientific manner as the so-called 'pure' sciences. This view of course sees human beings as being a part of the world, not somehow separate from it. Humans are of the world, so to speak, not just moving around in it.

Biological reductionism

Chapter Three examined reductionism. The very start of this chapter discussed levels of explanation. Here the important point relating to whether or not psychology can – or should – be a science was that the more reductionist levels (Figure 3.1) actually do lend themselves more readily to the objective investigation that the scientific method would typically adopt. The more holistic levels are somehow less tangible, that is, less easy to touch. They are less easy to locate in a particular point in space. As such, of course, anything that is difficult to pin down in terms of its spatial location is by definition difficult or impossible to examine as an 'object'. An example of what is meant here is provided in the following quotation from Rom Harré:

> If we were to shake hands, someone strolling by might ask: 'Now what are they up to?' The mere grasping of paws is something which perhaps is a biological inheritance, but *as people* [emphasis mine] we could be sealing a bet, or greeting each other, I could be congratulating you, we could be preparing for a boxing match. There are umpteen things people can be *doing* [emphasis mine] when they do the one biological thing 'touch paws'. Handshakes are psychologically effective in so far as they are interpreted. It is those interpretations . . . which create the social world. (Miller, 1983, p. 158)

At the lower levels, what is going on when two people shake hands can be easily observed, measured, recorded, etc. In other words, these lower levels lend themselves readily to objective investigation. The higher levels, however, are rather more difficult to 'get at'. At the immediately observable level, then, of course everyone knows what these two people are doing. They are shaking hands. But what are they really doing by shaking hands? What they are really doing is rather less easily observed. For shaking hands might mean different things. If the shaking of hands is interpreted and intended as a congratulation, then how would an objective and independent observer ever know this for sure? Such interpretation and intention is carried around, so to speak, in the heads of the people involved. Indeed at the more holistic social-psychological level, we are dealing with a reality which is far more elusive and hidden from an outside observer than the mere behaviour of shaking hands. The hidden and the elusive cannot really be the object of scientific endeavour. This 'elusiveness' of the social world is examined later in this chapter where the particular problems associated with social psychology are discussed.

Reductionism and the mind–body problem

Chapter Four examined the issue of reductionism with specific reference to the mind–body problem. If the mind is non-physical, or meta-physical, then how could it possibly be investigated by objective methods of scientific investigation? If the mind is not physical, then it cannot be located anywhere in space; therefore, it would literally be nowhere to be seen or observed, and seeing and observing are an all-important aspect of doing science. If, on the other hand, you argue, as many philosophers and psychologists now do, that all thoughts, feelings, sensations and emotions have a physical basis, then all of these psychological realities would indeed logically be available to scientific investigation. These would be available, some would argue, if only we had the right technology to investigate them. It could be that this availability, however, is more possible in principle than in practice. To put this simply, there must logically be a biological basis for any individual's feelings and thoughts of, for example, regret or indecision, but how on earth is indecision or regret really going to be located through physiological probing of an individual's brain by a scientist? Nonetheless, many psychologists are attracted to the idea that eventually all problems and questions posed in psychology will be solved at the level of biology, physiology and ultimately at the atomic and sub-atomic level of physics. Bannister explains just why this attraction might be rather misguided:

> Reductionism, as it manifests itself amongst psychologists, is a philosophic posture which assumes that physiology is somehow nearer to reality than psychology and therefore a more 'basic science'. A concept such as 'neurone' is somehow seen as co-equivalent with a real event . . . while psychological concepts are thought of as somehow at a greater remove from reality. (Bannister, 1968, p. 231)

Let us briefly refer back to the example presented earlier concerning what people are really doing when they shake hands. Along the same lines as Bannister's point above, it could similarly be claimed that the physical or muscular behaviour which is readily observable when people shake hands is somehow a more 'real event' than the less tangible social implications that underlie the act itself. But the point is that when people are actually involved in shaking hands, they are engaged in a symbolic and meaningful act. Importantly, this is not just behaviour pure and simple; this is interpreted behaviour.

Prescriptive and descriptive laws

A distinction has been drawn (Chapter Two) between prescriptive and descriptive laws. Science is concerned with attempting to make true and precise descriptions about the nature of the world. Prescriptive laws on the other hand are really commands to do or not to do something. In the legal sense, 'prescriptive' literally means that what we should or should not do is *written down* beforehand by governing or legislative bodies.

Falsifiability

An example of a law of nature was given earlier: water always boils at 212° F at sea level. It is important to note that the careful wording here specifies that the boiling point varies with altitude. If the law simply stated that water boils at 212° F, this would not actually be a true statement. Any observer, sitting by the side of the sea, could mistakenly believe that they had confirmed by observation that the law was true. What is required is that the conditions need to be varied, by boiling water at other altitudes for example. Thus the philosopher Karl Popper suggested that to establish whether or not a law is true, what was required was that the scientist attempt vigorously to falsify a law, rather than just attempt to confirm it. Repeated failure to falsify provides more and more confidence that a law is actually likely to be true.

Analyse the extract from Sartre's novel *Nausea* below. Here the writer is making a clear distinction between *descriptions* of the natural world as it is, and the world as it is made or *prescribed* by governing bodies. Identify two examples of each.

Progress exercise

They come out of their offices after the day's work, they look at the houses and the squares with a satisfied expression, they think that it is their town. A 'good solid town'. They aren't afraid, they feel at home. . . . They are given proof, a hundred times a day, that everything is done mechanically, that the world obeys fixed, unchangeable laws. Bodies released in a vacuum all fall at the same speed, the municipal park is closed every day at four p.m. in winter, at six p.m. in summer, lead melts at 335° C, the last tram leaves the Town Hall at 11.05 p.m. . . . they think about Tomorrow, in other words simply about another today; towns have only one day at their disposal which comes back exactly the same every morning. They barely tidy it up a little on Sundays. (Sartre, 1965, p. 225)

The place of theory in science

Proposing or constructing a theory provides a means of tying together various observations about the world that have already been made. It also provides an ability to make predictions. Moreover theory can help to guide the scientist in terms of where to look in order to even start to make observations at all. If observations are made which are predicted by the theory itself, then it can be said that the theory has been supported, that it has been confirmed. The following example given by J. Hospers should help to illustrate the way in which an existing theory can direct observation:

> One of the most dramatic illustrations of this is the discovery of the planet Neptune. When the planet Uranus was discovered through telescopes in 1721, it was carefully observed; as time passed its orbit was charted – which turned out to be somewhat surprising. According to Newton's laws of motion, it should have been at position X at a certain time, but instead it was at position Y. Astronomers might have used this as evidence against Newton's theory. But the theory already explained such a wide range of phenomena that they were hesitant to do this – it seemed preferable to bet on a theory that already explained much rather than scrap it in the face of seemingly contrary evidence. Two astronomers, Adams and Leverrier (acting independently of one another), looked about for an explanation of the peculiarity which would be compatible with Newton's theory: namely that there was a hitherto unobserved planet that was exerting a gravitational pull on Uranus. The two astronomers assumed the truth of Newtonian mechanics, and on the basis of it, plus their observations of Uranus, calculated the position of the hitherto undiscovered planet. . . . But in Einstein's theory of relativity a new theory emerged, not replacing Newton's but leading to different observable consequences at some points. If Einstein's view was correct, that light must be attracted to heavy bodies, then light coming from a star . . . if travelling close to the sun, must be deflected by the gravitational pull of the sun. This could not normally be confirmed because the light of the sun makes it impossible for us to see stars in the daytime. But during a total eclipse of the sun, the difference in position should be observable. The stars near the sun were photographed in the total solar eclipse of May 29, 1919, and the observations confirmed Einstein's theory. Again a prediction had been made on the basis of the theory, and its success was among the factors that led to its acceptance. (Hospers, 1990, pp. 169–170)

The place of theory in psychology

Both Newton's and Einstein's theories could be described as 'grand theories' because they could successfully predict so much. It could be argued that behaviourism was a grand theory because it claimed that it would eventually explain everything concerning human behaviour in terms of associative learning. Not all theoretical statements, however, are quite so all-encompassing. The following examples illustrate this.

(a) The blindsight studies

The phenomenon concerning human vision which is referred to as Blindsight (Weiskrantz, 1986) was predicted as theoretically possible because of physiological observations that had already been made. These observations included the physiological fact that there are at least six branches of the optic nerve that terminate in the midbrain and in other sub-cortical regions. One of these branches, containing around 100,000 fibres, is in no way a trivial pathway as this is actually larger than the entire auditory nerve. Patients with specific damage to particular parts of the visual cortex would be blind in the corresponding part of their visual field. Weiskrantz believed that theoretically such patients should, despite their blindness in particular parts of the field, be able to process visual information presented within these 'blind' regions. He believed this because it was reasonable to assume that the pathways that terminated in areas other than the cortex must serve some kind of visual function. It was this theoretical proposition that led to the discovery of the fact that processing of visual information in 'blind' areas was indeed possible. Although patients reported that they could not 'see' in these areas in the conventional way that we talk about seeing, they were, however, able to point to the exact location within the 'blind' part of the field where, for example, a light was flashed. They were also able to behave appropriately in response to visual stimuli and were capable of doing this even though they experienced no conscious awareness of them.

(b) Hemispheric specialisation concerning language functions

It is generally accepted that the left hemisphere is specialised for language functions for the majority of people. However, neurologists and psychologists theorised that there may well be some difference concerning lateralisation in people who speak more than one language. It must be noted that such theorising itself can never be directly tested or confirmed. Rather, specific experimental observations must be made which test specific hypotheses. In this example it is immediately apparent that a direct and testable hypothesis would have to be formulated. How else could psychologists investigate something as complex as laterality of function with respect to language? One procedure for investigating this question involves asking participants to tap keys with their fingers. They are also asked to speak or to read at the same time. The hypothesis here is that speakers of just one language would be able to tap more frequently when asked to use their left fingers whilst speaking than when asked to speak whilst using their right fingers. The logic being that because the left hemisphere controls the right-hand part of the body, there would be more interference with finger-tapping when speaking or reading when using the right hand as compared with using the left hand. This is a question of 'competition' for the capacities of the left hemisphere. The consequent hypothesis would be that if bilinguals did in fact have right hemisphere participation when producing or processing language, then their finger-tapping rates are likely to be affected for both the left and the right hand. Thus, for example, Soares (1984) did indeed find this to be the case.

Objectivity in science

Visual illusions provide clear evidence that true objectivity is not really possible. Kanizsa's triangle (Figure 6.2) illustrates that rather than being able to see objectively what is there waiting to be observed on the page, the observer's perception is driven by an effort to make sense of the visual data. This effort to make sense often involves expectations and beliefs about the stimulus, or, as in this case at least, an interpretation of what the stimulus is likely to represent. Interpretation also involves the observer calling upon what s/he already knows about the world. This problem concerning objectivity is not confined to psychology. Other disciplines also encounter their own particular difficulties. In social anthropology, for example, observation of the behaviour of people in other cultures can so easily fall into an inappropriate comparison with the things that we already know about our own culture. For example, it might be tempting to explain the meaning inherent in rituals in the observer's own terms. Later sections of this chapter underline the argument that social 'worlds' are not 'things' that await direct observation. Rather, they are only properly known by full membership of and immersion in the culture itself. Observation requires membership of a particular 'world', not detached onlooking.

Another discipline that encounters problems with objectivity is history. The historian may well carefully piece together facts, but all facts are selected facts. As such the endeavour inevitably involves bias. A mistaken belief held by many is that a biologist looking through a microscope somehow sees something that constitutes a real and direct observation: a direct observation because there it is. It's right before our eyes to see through the microscope. The problem is that looking through a microscope is usually 'theory-laden'. This is to say that there is usually an incredible amount of theory behind microscopic observation which informs the scientists as to exactly what it might be that is being observed. In 'new physics' there is the widespread belief that the observer is always an integral part of what is actually observed; Einstein's Law of relativity is concerned with this truism. The observer can never really stand outside of the thing that is under observation. In fact, the very observation itself is generally acknowledged to change that which is being observed. In Chapter Four, for example, the point was made that a thermometer actually changes the temperature of a glass of water when immersed into it. Moreover, different measuring apparatus will 'trap' a different aspect of the world.

Similarly, psychologists are probably in even more danger of changing that which they are observing by the very act of observation. Simply being there to make the observations adds an undesirable social dimension to the situation. In an experiment on memory, for example, the participant may try to perform well in order to impress the experimenter, may be under-motivated to do well because the experimenter reminds them of someone they don't like, and so on.

Why have so many psychologists been so concerned with making psychology a scientific discipline?

The objective methods of the pure sciences have had a most remarkable success during the last one hundred or so years. Incredible technological advances have been made possible only by the rigorous application of scientific investigation, involving prediction and control over the world, and a thorough grasp of how the world works in terms of causation. This, in itself, is impressive.

It is little wonder that psychologists were attracted to the idea of gaining respect for psychology by 'making a science' out of it. If the achievements of science are themselves so very impressive, it is worth noting that there is another good reason why people are so in awe of science. This reason is that a distinction can be drawn between what might be called subjective and objective knowledge within science itself. For example, assume that you wish to take a plane from London to Rome. Well, one thing is for certain here: the scientific knowledge exists to allow you to do that. Flights leave every day from London for Rome. It is an everyday, common occurrence which can be taken for granted. The necessary knowledge to fly you to Rome exists, but where exactly is this knowledge? Who possesses it? Well, the pilot knows certain things about how to fly the aircraft. S/he probably knows quite a lot, but not everything, about how the plane actually works. The engineers who built the plane all know different things. However, it is probable, if not almost certain, that not one of them knows absolutely everything necessary to build a plane that will actually fly. One engineer might specialise in hydraulics, another in fuels or electrics, and so on. A lot of people know a lot of things subjectively (i.e. personally), but no one individual knows enough to build a plane to fly you from London to Rome; however, the objective knowledge required exists 'out there', so to speak, and is used every single day.

It is easy to see from this example that really everyone is somewhat in awe of what objectively is known. Even the hydraulics engineer or the fuel expert, with their own specific knowledge, has to place trust in the idea that the total objective knowledge required exists. No one individual knows enough to get a plane built and then flown successfully from A to B. However, we humans have achieved this feat together with many other scientific accomplishments. No wonder, then, that most people seem to have such great respect for science, scientists included.

So, in view of this sense of awe and respect, it is hardly surprising that psychology has attempted to 'ape' the pure sciences; however, this is seen by many psychologists as inappropriate and unhelpful. Here Harré ridicules such attempts to gain respectability for psychology:

> When psychologists first began to try to be scientists they were like a young man setting off to be a novelist who grows a beard,

buys a typewriter, who dresses up and adopts the superficial manners of the literary world as he imagines them. Psychologists talked like physical scientists, they called their results 'measures', they decorated their learned papers with tables of numbers, and they even tried their hand at a little rather simple mathematics. It was just dressing up. Somehow the essence of the scientific enterprise eluded them. (Miller, 1983, p. 157)

Indeed Harré not only believed that the scientific approach was unhelpful, he went so far as to urge psychologists to avoid the inevitable objectification and depersonalisation of the scientific method. To do this he suggested that it would be a good idea 'to treat people as human beings'. The next section examines this suggestion in terms of the implications for the way in which people are viewed in psychiatry.

Scientific objectification and its implications for psychiatry

In his classic text, *The Divided Self*, the so-called 'anti-psychiatrist' R. D. Laing set out to protest against the scientific depersonalisation of schizophrenics. Here he objects to the tendency to concentrate upon the patient as a complex physical-chemical system which has 'gone wrong' rather than as a person who is experiencing distressing psychological difficulties. He makes the important point that the patient is actually both of these things. The patient indeed is both of these things depending upon the attitude of the observer, and the attitude adopted is the result of an intentional act on the part of the observer.

Now, if you are sitting opposite me, I can see you as another person like myself; without you changing or doing anything differently, I can now see you as a complex physical-chemical system, perhaps with its own idiosyncrasies but chemical none the less for that; seen in this way, you are no longer a person but an organism. . . . Seen as an organism, man cannot be anything else but a complex of things, of its, and the processes that ultimately comprise an organism are it-processes . . . the theory of man as person loses its way if it falls into an account of man as a machine or man as an organismic system of it-processes. The converse is also true. (Laing, 1959, pp. 21–22)

Laing is really arguing here that as soon as the psychologist or the psychiatrist views the patient with the traditional scientific attitude, then it becomes impossible to view the patient as a person. And vice versa. This echoes Bannister's comments in his paper 'The myth of physiological psychology', ' . . . the chances of developing a science of physiological psychology are about as good (or as bad) as the chances of developing a chemical sociology or a biological astronomy' (Bannister, 1968, p. 229).

Laing argues that a scientific approach to the person is really a contradiction in terms, and importantly he reminds us of the inevitable depersonalisation of the patient whenever the psychiatrist adopts a stance which is purely clinical, detached, objective, scientific, medical, systematic, and classifying. Laing, together with the other 'anti-psychiatrists' such as David Cooper, asserted that the stance adopted should be quite the opposite: involved, inter-subjective – listening to what the patient was actually saying, rather than looking for symptoms to assist in pigeon-holing and classification. He would insist that the medicalisation of people suffering from mental distress was not always appropriate and that the patient's family environment might hold the key as to why they are disturbed. Treating the patient as a person actually involved a rejection of trying to make a science out of psychiatry. As mentioned at the start of this chapter, science attempts to look for consistencies and generalisations in order to impose or describe a 'patterned' understanding of the way the world tends to work. Rather than dealing with generalities, Laing believed that each patient was to be viewed as a unique individual with unique and individual things to say to the world. Psychologists often refer to this unique approach as being **idiographic**. This term can easily be remembered by thinking of the related word *idiosyncratic*, a word which is often used to describe, for example, a particular individual's unique mannerisms and ways of behaving. Alternatively, the **nomothetic** approach implies the search for generalities and similarities between people. This term is derived from the Greek *nomos*, meaning *law*.

The above distinction provokes the following argument concerning the status of psychology as a science. Now, the point has already been made above that science implies a search for generalisations and consistencies. That is, a search for laws concerning the way in which the world works. Thus all science should really be described as being nomothetic. So, any psychologist wishing to study what is unique and individual about persons cannot be said to be 'doing' science. The inappropriate over-application of the scientific method in psychology is often referred to as an example of 'scientism'.

The idiographic approach could be said to be person-centred; whereas the nomothetic approach, with its emphasis upon *if . . . then* statements and observations, often resulting from observations via experiments, is variable-centred.

Science and social psychology

Reductionism and social psychology

Experimental reductionism was examined earlier and it is now necessary to examine an alternative approach. The so-called 'crisis' in social psychology is outlined and it is argued that experimental reductionism in this sub-division of psychology may well tease out important findings on how people behave in groups. For example, experimental studies highlight the tendency for larger groups to arrive at riskier more daring decisions than smaller groups (e.g. Stoner, 1961). This is a phenomenon often referred to as 'risky shift'. Not only are experimentally-based researchers here fairly sure that they have what is called internal validity but such research itself strongly and clearly suggests that further investigations should be made to establish whether or not the initial experimental findings can be 'mapped onto' the 'real world'. That is, does the research have external validity? What effects, for example, does the size of a jury have upon the kinds of decisions reached concerning the accused? Does an increase in the size of the jury also promote a tendency towards 'risky shift'? If not, then how quickly or slowly do different sizes of juries manage to come to their decisions? What are the implications of cost of the trial to the taxpayer? Hence, it could be argued that results from the reductionist – and hence highly controlled – environment of the social psychology laboratory can provide specific pointers for application to the less easily controlled real world.

On the other hand, it could and has been argued that the social 'world' is not really like a 'thing' that can be readily examined via the scientifically credible approach of the experimental method. This view suggests that the social world is continually in the process of being socially created and socially maintained and that to penetrate such processes really requires an approach which is far more subtle than simply performing an experiment. The next section examines this rather more subtle way of 'doing' social psychology. Some of the limitations of experimental reductionism will be explicitly and, at times, implicitly addressed.

Examining social reality: avoiding experimental reductionism

The elusiveness of 'social reality'

The so-called 'crisis' in social psychology was essentially a reaction against the experimental and inevitably reductionist approach. The argument concerned the idea that the only thing that the social psychologist actually observes when conducting experiments is how people behave when they are put into experimental situations. Here, then, the experimental reductionism inevitably leads to an analysis of how people behave when they are only required to 'play around' in an artificial 'mini-world' of the researcher's making. In 'playing around', just how involved are the participants? How vital to the participants is it that they really solve problems set, etc.? It is quite understandable that psychologists would wish to look at these rather more manageable 'mini-worlds'. After all, the 'real world' outside of the laboratory is much more complex. The two 'worlds' really do belong in different categories. 'Mini-worlds' can be examined discretely. This means that they can be examined all at once, so to speak. However, the 'real world' doesn't show itself so easily to the researcher. The world of 'social reality' is not a thing that can be examined and measured. Tables, trees, gardens and buildings – and indeed experimental set-ups – are all things that can be seen, touched, walked around, etc., and are things that lend themselves to being examined and measured.

The 'real world' outside of the laboratory does not have this 'thing-like' quality. Now, what does this imply? Well, one of the main features of what is being referred to here as the 'real world' is that this 'social reality' is carried around in the heads, so to speak, of the members of this very world. For here, we are concerned with the invisible social strings that bind groups of people together. We all know that during every day of our lives we are all involved in a web of social obligations and expectations. We have a sense of duty to preserve, and a sense of honour. For example, we may have previously caused someone some offence, and thus are engaged in the business of putting things right. Alternatively, we might ourselves have been offended or injured by another person and might be enmeshed in trying to get even. We might be driven by the desire to prove ourself. This socially-driven psychological force might be behind the efforts that we put into trying to pass an examination, or to do well and achieve good results in a new job. However, these social forces do not belong to the category of 'things' that can be readily observed, looked at, and measured. They exist at a rather more elusive level.

What do experiments really tell us?

It has been argued that the environment of the laboratory situation is deliberately reductionist. Moreover, that it is only within such simplified circumstances that experiments can actually be conducted. It is only by reducing the focus to strictly defined variables that it is possible to tease out what exactly affects what. How will manipulating the independent variable affect the dependent variable? This is the simplified question being asked when an experiment is conducted. Particular experimental variations can tease out subtle cause-and-effect relationships. This is what J. S. Mill referred to as the 'rule of one variable'. Only one thing at a time should be changed. In Milgram's obedience experiments, for example, participants often reported that they only obeyed because the experiments were conducted at the prestigious university, Yale. So, to apply Mill's rule, Milgram performed his experiments again. This time doing everything as before except that the location of where the experiments were conducted was changed. Hence, he repeated his experiments at a location away from the university, in the centre of town. He was, however, careful to do everything else exactly as he had done in the initial experiment. Indeed, it is only by operating in this manner that any investigator is able to draw conclusions about how the world actually works and to draw conclusions about what is really having an effect upon what. In this manner, the researcher attempts to draw out 'lawful relationships'.

It can be argued, however, that such lawful relationships only really exist in the laboratory. That outside of the laboratory, things are far more complex, and that it is this very complexity that suggests that what is observed under the restrictions of laboratory conditions cannot practically be translated or exported to the real world. For, in this real world, the variables that affect human beings are so numerous that it is difficult if not impossible to enter into any realistic cause–effect analysis. This cause–effect analysis is, of course, what constitutes the doing of science. Perhaps, then, it is impossible to expect that human behaviour can be examined 'scientifically'. Jung describes this difficulty thus:

> . . . we need the laboratory with its incisive restrictions in order to demonstrate the invariable validity of natural law. If we leave things to nature, we see a very different picture: every process is partially or totally interfered with by chance, so much so that under natural circumstances a course of events absolutely conforming to specific laws is almost an exception. (Jung, 1989, p. xxii)

Thus Jung suggests that it is only when the 'world' has been reduced to the artificiality of the experimental set-up that psychologists can start to examine the lawful principles which govern psychology. However, these principles which might so clearly apply in the laboratory, are rather more clouded in the complexity of the real world. This doesn't necessarily imply that the mechanistic principles of cause-and-effect do not apply when it comes to the realm of psychology. What it does imply is that the contributing factors that determine human behaviour and experience, i.e. the domain of study for the discipline of psychology, are so numerous that it is almost impossible to make predictions. It could be argued that a system may well be mechanistic, but also it is so complex that it is impossible to see what it is going to do next.

Consider the above paragraph again for one moment. Doesn't this sound a good argument for reductionism rather than against it? Does this not really underline the idea that it is only by simplifying the system under investigation that we can start properly to observe what is going on within it? In terms of trying to do science, is not the artificial simplicity of the unnatural setting of the laboratory much preferable to the complexity of the naturally occurring world?

Moreover, in further defence of the use of the reductionist environment of the experimental set-up, it could be argued that an indispensable and intrinsic part of conducting experiments in the first place is that the researcher makes sure that participants are randomly allocated to experimental conditions. This is done to ensure that any chance factors (as described by Jung above) that find their way from the 'real world' and into the laboratory-based experiment will be allocated as evenly as possible across experimental conditions. By doing this, the researcher can be fairly sure that any cause-and-effect (IV–DV) relationships are not in fact simply due to **sampling error**. Rather that they are actually to do with changes in the independent variable. When studying memory, for example, the experimenter might have a group of 20 participants, and these participants will vary in their ability to remember. These variations are due to a multitude of factors: participants will vary in intelligence; motivation to perform well for the experimenter; apprehension of actually having their memory tested; how tired or energetic they feel at the time, and so on. Random allocation to the experimental conditions will, statistically speaking, tend thereby to randomly distribute all of these complicating factors. An alternative to this method of **randomisation** is that of **counter-balancing**.

Arguments for and against experimental reductionism: a case study from social psychology

Ebbesen and Konečni (1975) investigated an important problem related to the 'real world'. They wished to examine what factors were taken into account when judges make bail recommendations. The work of these researchers is discussed in some detail later in this chapter. First, however, we need to remember that when a defendant is accused of a crime, the process of Law assumes that the defendant is innocent until proven guilty; there is usually a time lapse of some months between the arrest and trial; and the previous two points imply that to hold the defendant in jail for the time period between arrest and trial might ultimately be seen to be wrong or inhuman if that defendant is finally found to be innocent of the crime and thus acquitted at the end of the trial.

Bail, of course, is an amount of money paid by the defendant which provides some degree of guarantee that s/he will turn up to appear in court at the start of the trial. Non-appearance meaning that the money is forfeited. This ensures that the defendant has a strong motivation to appear. Now, what factors are generally considered to be taken into account by a judge when coming to a decision whether to allow bail or keep the defendant in prison until the trial? These are primarily: **(i)** the seriousness of the offence that the defendant is accused of;

(ii) the defendant's past record; **(iii)** the perceived dangerousness of the defendant (whether the defendant is likely to commit a similarly serious crime if let out on bail); **(iv)** the extent to which the defendant has 'community ties' (what is meant here is the extent to which the defendant has a job, spouse, family, home, etc. in the country under whose laws he is accused. If accused in the USA the question might address his 'community ties' within the *State* that he is accused); **(v)** the amount of money demanded of (or offered by) the defence.

Obviously the investigation by Ebbesen and Konečni concerned a very serious issue. Their research is useful here because they made use of both an experimental simulation concerning bail-setting and naturalistic observation of judges actually making bail decisions.

Some details regarding Ebbesen and Konečni (1975)

Taking advantage of the benefits of the reductionist setting of the experimental simulation, the researchers invented case studies about imaginary defendants. They were thus able to manipulate and control the independent variables and then see what effect these had upon the dependent variable. (The dependent variable, of course, was whether or not the judge granted bail for the imaginary case.) The four independent variables that they manipulated were:

(1) the amount of money recommended by the prosecution;
(2) the amount recommended by the defence;
(3) whether or not the accused had a criminal record; and
(4) whether or not the accused had community ties.

The advantage of the experimental simulation is that by reducing down to four comparatively straightforward variables, the researchers were able to create their imaginary cases by combining them in every way possible. The point being that by doing this in such a neat manner, they were able to establish very clearly which factors, and in which combinations, the judges considered most important when considering bail applications. In this way, the independent effect of each could be clearly established. What the researchers actually established was that each factor did have an effect. Furthermore, they established that whether or not the defendant had community ties was the factor that most influenced whether or not the judge granted bail.

So far so good. The above simulation seems to show neatly what the cause-and-effect factors are when judges consider bail applications. By reducing the set-up to this clear-cut and straightforward set of variables, the researchers were able to demonstrate similarly clear-cut relationships about what affects what when judges consider bail applications. Important here is the fact that the judges do seem to be taking into account the factors that are generally agreed upon as being the important indicators that an accused will or will not appear in court on the date of the trial itself. The researchers' approach here, then, would seem to provide a good argument for this type of experimental simplification or reductionism.

Unfortunately, there is a counter-argument. Having conducted this simulation, the researchers then followed five of the judges around in the real world. (They had used some 18 judges in the simulation study.) They did so to observe what the judges actually did in real cases where bail was being considered. In the naturalistic setting, of course, the researchers had access to all relevant details about the accused. But, in the natural world, things are rather less clear-cut than in the imaginary world of the simulation. The independent variables are not so carefully calibrated or finely tuned. That is, they are confounded. Additionally, it was found that in real-world applications for bail, the judges seemed to pay little or no attention to community ties. This was in direct contradiction to the findings of the simulation where such ties were seen to be the strongest causal factor as to whether or not bail was granted.

The simulation study seemed at first quite attractive. Here we can be sure about causal relationships between variables. Unfortunately, this simulation might simply be a good illustration of what was suggested earlier in this chapter. Namely, that in order to do any experimental study, we simply have to operationalise variables. The danger being that the variables chosen don't actually turn out to be significant to the people under investigation. As it would appear, the judges under investigation in the naturalistic observations appeared to be involved in something far more complex than simply weighing up a few variables such as community ties, and the amount demanded by the prosecution, etc. In fact, what they seemed in reality to be involved in was a social interaction with the prosecution attorney. The proper model to describe what was *really* going on did not concern the variables described. Rather it had to do with social dynamics with those bringing the prosecution. This dynamic involving attempts at persuasion and influence concerning the judge's ultimate decision as to whether or not to grant bail:

> The Social influence model (from the real-life data) suggests that the bail arraignment is, like the trial itself, a kind of adversarial procedure, a contest between attorneys . . . The simulation data suggest that the bail hearing is what it is supposed to be, a weighting by the judge of many facts about the defendant that will affect the likelihood of his appearing for trial. (Brown, 1986, p. 256)

Conclusions to be drawn from this research

What conclusions can be drawn concerning experimental reductionism from the above example? Well, on the one hand, the experimental part of this study gives a clear account of the relative importance of the various factors, as perceived by the judges, concerning an accused's likelihood of eventually appearing in court to stand trial should bail actually be granted. It is worth repeating here that the researchers seemed to discover that judges do appear to follow agreed guide-lines concerning the importance of community ties and the other factors generally regarded as good indicators as to whether or not the accused is likely to appear in court: a correct process of weighing up the 'cold facts' surrounding the case in question.

On the other hand, the naturalistic observation revealed other things. Notably, that considerations of applications for bail seemed to be taken over by the social processes of persuasion. Here there was a danger that strong arguments on the part of defence and prosecution counsel took over. In brief, that the whole process was not at all the detached and calm weighing-up of the facts that it was supposed to be. There is a clear indication here that both methods of investigation were of great importance. Moreover, that the results from both methods can be taken together in order to arrive at sensible recommendations to the legal profession concerning how it should go about hearing applications for bail.

When is an artificial setting also natural?

The Ebbesen and Konečni experiment focused upon the limitations and advantages of the experimental method. The restrictions of the artificial set-up of the experiment provided obvious advantages with respect to identifying cause-and-effect relationships, but the naturalistic observation was important in demonstrating that judges did not actually appear to be doing what they claimed they did. Here, then, the problem concerned *external validity*. What was going on under laboratory conditions did not resemble what actually happened in the outside world, that is, in the 'real world' outside of – or external to – the laboratory. There are some situations in 'real life', however, that can be studied quite easily in the laboratory without too much fear about external validity. There are some situations that are always artificial set-ups: in identity parades, eye-witnesses will view a line-up of individuals in order to see whether or not they can recognise the person who attacked them, for example. Such line-ups are themselves not necessarily what might be called 'naturally occurring'. On the contrary, they are contrived aspects of police procedure. Identity parades can be said to possess many of the qualities of a laboratory set-up. Furthermore, they can be said to do so because the witness is taken into a strange environment within an institution where the test of their memory will take place. The witness is likely to feel somewhat apprehensive; under pressure to perform well and to make a successful identification; and in fact, they are likely to feel very much like any participant turning up at a university to take part in an experiment conducted by a psychologist.

The above paragraph proposes that the witness attending an identity parade *and* the participant (in an experimental set-up) are both likely to feel that they are in a contrived and artificial situation. As such, it could be argued that psychological investigations in terms of examining factors associated with identity parades should go ahead without too much concern with regard to external validity. But perhaps this is just an exception because concerns about external validity remain a real issue in many areas of psychology. Indeed, the research by Ebbesen and Konečni clearly illustrates this very problem.

Review exercise

The place of theory in science
Re-read the section 'The place of theory in science' which covers the way in which Neptune was discovered. What were the observations made concerning the movement of the planets which led to the prediction of the existence of Neptune? Now read the section which follows this concerning the 'Blindsight studies'. How did theory guide Weiskrantz's experiments regarding the 'blindsight' phenomenon? In other words, what physiological observations had already been made which made blindsight a theoretical possibility?

Summary

Arguments for and against the idea that psychology could or should adopt the 'scientific' approach have been presented in this chapter. It is quite easy to see why psychologists have often tried to follow the methods of the 'pure' sciences because of the enormous technological successes that physics, chemistry and biology have achieved. But whether or not it is *appropriate* to do so is another matter. The so-called 'qualitative–quantitative' issue was commented on in Chapter One. There it was noted that the issue concerning subjectivity and objectivity is central to this question. Perhaps psychologists have been rather too obsessed with trying to be objective. Human beings do possess psychological states. These states include a whole range of things including thoughts, emotions and feelings, and all of these are very private and subjective phenomena. Hence, they are not really as easily scientifically observed as other phenomena in the world.

However, as with many of the debates in psychology, the answer to this question probably has to take the form of a sensible compromise. Psychology is an extremely broad discipline. It is therefore probably wise to conclude that the approach taken depends upon exactly which area of psychology is under investigation.

Further reading

Hospers, J. (1990) *An Introduction to Philosophical Analysis*, 3rd edn, London: Routledge. Chapter 4: 'Scientific knowledge'.

Hunt, M. (1993) *The Story of Psychology*, London: Anchor Books. This text would be of particular interest for study beyond A-level. For a comprehensive historical account of the various attempts to establish psychology as a science, refer to 'Part two: Founders of a new science'.

Gross, R. D. (1995) *Themes, Issues & Debates in Psychology*, London: Hodder & Stoughton. Chapter 11: 'Psychology as a science'.

6

The nature–nurture debate

What is it about?

The nature–nurture debate concerns the extent to which biological inheritance – nature – as compared to environmental factors – nurture – shape the individual. Environmental factors include personal experience and circumstances; the effects of learning and the impact of the social and political background into which an individual is born.

This issue is also sometimes referred to as the 'heredity–environment' controversy. An example of this would be the dispute between those such as Noam Chomsky who argue that individuals are born with a 'language acquisition device', or *LAD*, and those who maintain that it is a mistake to assume that the system for language acquisition is so deeply innate. The latter, of course, would argue that learning principles more probably apply. The former group argue that the *LAD* (also referred to as *LAS*, meaning 'language acquisition system') proposes an innate knowledge of a general, or universal, 'pool' (or system) of underlying rules of grammar that do not need to be learned. Here, the only part that experience – nurture or environment – plays is that the *actual language* that the individual happens to acquire depends upon where in the world s/he actually grows up. According to this theory, the individual selects from this universal pool those rules of grammar that apply to the particular language to which s/he is exposed.

Previous discussions

The nature–nurture debate is discussed in several places in this text. Behaviourists such as Skinner and Watson (Chapter Seven) put forward an extreme viewpoint that strongly proposes environmental determinism. Their view was one that saw the nurturing aspects as being of absolute importance. All behaviour was seen as being directly shaped and controlled through associative learning. The systems of reward and punishment in the animal's environment were the determining factors. Likewise, in human behaviour such systems of reward and punishment are to be found within the individual's immediate micro-environment such as family and school. They are also present within more politically-driven macro-environments at a national or cultural level.

Biological determinism was examined in the debate concerning the extent to which it can be said that we have free will (Chapter Two). Examples were given of the ways in which the nature of the biological system that we are born with dictates our own particular psychological make-up. For example, extraversion and introversion were seen as being directly controlled and determined by an individual's level of cortical arousal; in other words, they were seen as a result of an individual's nature.

The section towards the end of Chapter Three on the evolutionary perspective also comes down heavily on the side of nature. Here it is proposed that all behaviour is ultimately driven by the biological imperative – or command – that the individual must survive and pass on his or her genes.

In Chapter Four the various positions on the mind–body issue were discussed. *Materialism* proposed that mental events *are* physical events, whilst *epiphenomenalism* asserted that mental states are a product of physical events originating in the brain. Both of these positions imply the importance of nature, that is, the importance of the physical brain with which an individual is born. Later in this chapter, however, it will be argued that the quality or efficiency of the brain – and hence what we might call the 'mind' – must also be seen to be the end-product of an interaction of this inherited biology (nature) and the environmental factors (nurture) to which the individual is exposed. For example, environmental factors, such as an enriching and stimulating education and a balanced nutritional diet, are proposed as important in terms of nurturing (to best effect) what nature has provided.

Chapter Five asks the question as to whether or not psychology can be a science. One of the central issues concerns the place of human beings in the natural world. If humans are viewed as part of the world – rather than simply being *in* it – then it might be seen as appropriate to adopt the scientific approach that has been so successful in the natural sciences: finding the cause-and-effect relationships that determine how the world works. If this approach really is suitable for psychology, then it could be argued that the project for psychologists concerns an examination of the role of differing environmental and biological factors in individuals' subsequent behaviour and experience. That is, it concerns the effects of nurture and nature respectively. Included in this project is, inevitably, an appraisal of the ways in which the two combine.

Social constructionism

At conception there are a number of ways in which it could be argued that our nature is fixed. For example, it's just a fact that human beings cannot choose to do anything other than experience the world largely through vision, any more than bats cannot choose to use sound in order to know and navigate their way around this world. The scope of the visual system is also fixed in that it can only deal with a certain limited range of the electromagnetic spectrum. X-ray and infra-red cannot be directly processed and experienced except with the aid of special equipment such as the infra-red seeing devices used by the military. However, at birth an individual is not only propelled into a particular body, thrust into a specific biological 'prison' to be inhabited unto death, s/he is also thrown into a particular environment, into a particular social and political set of circumstances. From birth onwards, the child learns to adapt to the specific demands of this environment. It could be argued that the child is programmed biologically to make this adaptation, designed by nature to 'tune into' other people and into the social expectations dictated by cultural and political demands. Particularly, it could be argued that the child is 'programmed' by nature to interact appropriately with significant carers such as parents. However strong this thrust of nature, the nurture side of the argument must also be discussed.

The term *social constructionism* relates to the variability of the specific social and political environment that an individual is born into. The environments of humans are variable simply because they are constructed in the first place, rather than the direct product of nature. A variety of political systems and social arrangements exist throughout the world. We humans are certainly programmed by our very nature to live in social arrangements, that is to say, we are 'programmed' to co-exist with groups of other people. We are highly social animals, as are chimpanzees. Ants too operate in a most sophisticated social meshing of inter-activity and co-operation. The important difference between ants and humans, however, is that the social set-up for ants is *invariant* and automatically fixed by their nature; whereas within humans the biological imperative, or command, to form social groups can result in a wide range of social and political set-ups. It should be clear at this point that the social system into which a person is born must itself be described as a social construction.

The effects of the politically constructed environment on the individual

Social constructionism is a term that is frequently called upon to account for those socially and politically created environmental factors that affect people's psychological make-up in particular ways. Clearly such factors can be described as part of an individual's nurturing, one aspect of their environment.

To illustrate just how social constructions can influence an individual's psyche, consider the way in which personal attitudes and beliefs towards other groups of people are formed. Attitudes towards homosexuality, people of different ethnic backgrounds, gender, religions, having sex and children outside of marriage, tend generally – officially at least – to be more enlightened than they were say a century ago. But this relative enlightenment didn't occur because one day we all woke up and just adopted more constructive attitudes. (This is not to suggest that many individual people did not privately have the will for attitudes to change.) It occurred because of the introduction of legislation and political policy that outlawed, amongst other things, sexual and racial discrimination. Due to such political moves, then, a different set of values and attitudes was constructed, a different 'world' was put in place, so to speak. It is a truism to suggest that an enormously important part of our psyche – our opinions and beliefs – is the result of what is allowable and promoted within the particular environment into which we are born and within which we live our lives.

Can historical factors influence the psyche of a whole nation?

The particular point in history into which a person is born can also be said to shape their psychological make-up and hence to drive their behaviour. A dramatic example of this is the terrorist activities of the so-called Baader-Meinhof group in Germany in the early 1970s. (See, for example, Becker, 1977.) This political group took its name from the two young activists Andreas Baader and Ulrike Meinhof. If today you were to ask people whether or not they supported acts of terrorism against their own country, they would be most likely to say that such violent acts are wrong, destructive and ultimately futile. However, most young adults in Germany actually had some sympathy towards the activities of the Baader-Meinhof group. The activists themselves certainly believed in what they were doing. Even though what they were doing included bomb attacks against military bases, shopping complexes, the national press, and other targets. They also funded their operations by various criminal means including bank raids. So just why did such activities gain so much support? One psychoanalytic explanation for the Baader-Meinhof phenomenon proposes that these terrorists were symbolically attacking their fathers by making these attacks upon their own 'Fatherland'. This symbolic attack driven – consciously or unconsciously – by feelings of guilt about the atrocities perpetrated by their own fathers during World War II. This guilt in turn fuelled by further feelings of embarrassment and shame at the fact that West Germany had prospered since the end of the war in 1945. Indeed it had undergone what was referred to as the 'economic miracle'. Thus the feeling amongst young people was that Germany had prospered undeservedly, that it had become wealthy despite its dreadful recent past. This psychological explanation serves as a forceful argument that the psyche of an entire nation of young people (or at least *most* of them) can be shaped by the period in history into which they were born. This of course would constitute a forceful example of environmental determinism.

An example of 'nurturing out' what is natural

One further example follows to underline the way in which behaviour is subject to influence from socially constructed environments. Consider the fact that there is medical evidence to suggest that there are distinct advantages, including the helpful effects of gravity, in a woman giving birth with the trunk of her body in a vertical position (Russell, 1982). Moreover historical evidence suggests that such a position has been widely adopted throughout the ages. So why do most Western women adopt the supine delivery position? The answer is simply because that is the way women are expected in Western cultures to give birth. A clear-cut example of social constructionism if ever there was one. For here it is clear that the geographic location and historical era into which a woman is herself born can influence the way in which she is likely to give birth herself. In terms of the nature–nurture argument, this is a clear example of the more natural delivery position being shelved or 'nurtured out' simply because of cultural expectations.

Language and thought

There can be no doubt that humans are biologically pre-programmed to tune into 'natural language'. The term natural language refers to the spoken language of everyday conversations as opposed to the languages employed by computer programmers, mathematicians, or by writers of music. Our use of natural language can be regarded as the main thing that makes us so special. Other animals communicate with each other, but they do so in a rather limited and usually stereotyped way. Our natural ability to acquire language allows the production of an infinite number of novel and unique sentences. Moreover, these sentences convey an infinite number of ideas and concepts. This is an important point because it implies that a child is pre-programmed to develop the ability to understand sentences that have never been heard before. This is a strong argument for the nature side of the argument concerning the acquisition of language because it implies that there is more to attaining language abilities than mere imitation or reinforcement.

Discovering the rules of grammar: the role of nature

On the other hand, Skinner's fiercely argued environmentalism would propose that language is *entirely* learned and is, therefore, the result of nurture rather than nature. However, the limitations of Skinner's emphasis on nurture should be obvious. Certainly a child can be rewarded with praise for linking the correct word with the appropriate object, but this is really only a trivial aspect of what is actually involved in acquiring language. For example, children spontaneously employ grammatical rules without ever being formally taught what the rules are. Indeed children typically over-employ such rules. In doing so they make revealing 'errors' which underline that a rule has been acquired. A child might say 'I doed that yesterday'. Such an error indicates that this particular exception to the rule has not yet been incorporated by the child. It could be said that the exceptions are indeed learned through reinforcement and imitation – nurture – but that the child is geared by natural endowment to spontaneously discover what the rules of a particular language actually are. In this case, of course, the rule acquired is that 'ed' is added to the verb to form the past tense. For example, *I play* becomes *I played*. An exception to this, which would need to be learned, would be that the past tense of *I do* becomes *I did*.

Language: the role of nurture

The nurture side of the argument here, however, concerns the actual language to which the child is exposed. In discussing the relationship between language and thought, the philosopher Wittgenstein proposed that it is only through language that we can and do think. He proposed that the limits of his 'world' were dictated by the limits of the particular language that he had acquired. An example of this would be that in English temporal and spatial concepts are mixed together when we say, 'I am going to be away for a long time'. Time is experienced as being spatial and linear in nature, in other words, time is conceived of (or thought about) as if it were like a road along which we travel. For example, when talking about the passing of time relating to our own personal history, the expression 'life's journey' is often used.

Logically it would be argued that speakers of other languages that do not talk about time in spatial terms would experience time in a different manner. Another example is that English has very few words for snow: these might include the words slush or blizzard. Obviously snow is quite an important aspect of life for Eskimos. They have over twenty different words that distinguish at once between slush, packed snow, flaky snow, drifting snow, etc.; hence over twenty different types of snow are talked about and indeed experienced. That is to say that these different types of snow are perceived as such because the language directs the perceptual processes. The language and the perception are directly linked. Wittgenstein would claim that such differences in the languages actually dictate differences in how the world is perceived. Here language and thought or perception are not only linked, the language *is* the thought. In the context of the nature–nurture debate, then, what is being proposed here is that the particular language to which the individual is exposed will determine the way in which the individual will come to experience and perceive the world.

This nurture side of the argument is often referred to as 'linguistic relativity'. However, one objection to the idea that the language is the thought is that if there is no thought without language, then this would seem to make a mystery of how a child comes to acquire language in the first place. It would seem to ignore the necessary fact that the child must be interacting intelligently with and making sense of language from the very start. Admittedly, without language we cannot talk about our thoughts and ideas, we cannot convey concepts, etc. However, it does not logically follow that no mental life at all exists without language. For example, other 'candidates' for what is involved in thinking involve the use of visual imagery, etc.

On the nurture side of the argument, studies with babies highlight the importance of the actual language that the developing child is exposed to. Goswami (2000), for example, reports on research which shows that exposure to a particular language actually alters the brain. At around ten months of age, a Japanese baby has become unable to differentiate between the sound of the words 'lake' and 'rake'. At seven months of age the same baby has no difficulty. This is because the brain develops in such a way as to tune into the sound patterns which are important in the Japanese language. Obviously, an English-speaking baby's brain matures in such a way as to become 'wired' to pick up the above sound difference, because in English this discrimination is important. Thus, babies are born with brains that possess the innate ability to tune into whatever language they are exposed to. The particular language itself can be described as an environmental factor – nurture – that interacts with the brain's natural 'plasticity'. This term is used to describe the potential that the brain has to be shaped or changed in order to adapt to specific environments.

The above example provides a good illustration of the importance of both nature and nurture in terms of language acquisition. What should be evident here is the fact that an *interaction* takes place between heredity and environment. The adaptability of the brain to a particular environment is underlined in this example.

Instinct versus learning: ethological studies

The nature–nurture debate inevitably involves an examination of the extent to which behaviour is driven by instinct as opposed to learning. Psychologists have studied animals in two major ways: whereas behaviourists typically examined rats and pigeons under laboratory conditions, ethological studies involve the observation of animals in their natural habitat. Through such naturalistic observation, some dramatic examples of behaviours that strongly illustrate the powerful pre-programmed role of instinct have been discovered. Particular stimuli are known to produce automatic stereotyped behavioural responses. The stimulus-response might be quite simple. For example the red underbelly of the stickleback is a visual stimulus that produces behaviour associated with the defence of territory in another stickleback; and the young herring-gull pecks at the beak of its parent which automatically causes the parent to regurgitate food which it has collected.

Other responses are rather more complex and have been referred to as *fixed action patterns* in that the behaviour is always the same. It always takes the same form and the same sequence, and it is said to be 'ballistic' in that, once the behaviour is set in motion, it will continue through the whole sequence and cannot be interrupted. Important to the nature–nurture debate is the fact that such behaviours are universally present in all members of a defined class of a species irrespective of the animal's own particular experience. Hence animals reared in isolation still exhibit the behaviour. This indicates that the behaviour is not learned and is a pre-programmed instinct. Some insects, for example the digger wasp, take food back to the underground nest and place it just in front of the entrance. The insect first goes down into the nest to ensure that there is a clear route or passage, then reappears, collects the food and takes it down into the nest. Researchers have illustrated just how rigid this sequence of behaviour can be by pulling the food back a little further away from the nest entrance whilst the insect is in the nest 'checking' the passage. When this is done the insect reappears, pulls the food back to the original position, goes down again to 'check' and then reappears to collect the food. If the food is pulled back away from the nest entrance continuously by the researcher, the insect will get caught in a behavioural loop from which it cannot be released and will incessantly go through the same rigid sequence of behaviours.

Examples of the interaction of nature and nurture

However remarkably pre-programmed such behaviours might be, they are often also mediated by experience. For this reason, the nature–nurture issue is more complex than these examples of instinct-driven behaviour might at first suggest. For instance, the building of nests by birds and insects requires an extremely complex series of nest-building behaviours. Research conducted to examine the possible role of learning through imitation has involved rearing in isolation. Gould and Gould (1998) found that:

> . . . individuals reared in isolation will nonetheless select appropriate nest sites, gather suitable material and fashion it into the kind of nest that wild-reared individuals of the species create. True, nest building often improves with practice and site selection benefits from experience, but the basic elements are in place before the animal sets to work. Indeed, it is possible that the kinds of complex adaptive behaviour that so impress us are just the types of behaviour that must be innate, simply because they would be impossible to learn from scratch. (Gould and Gould, 1998)

Another example of the idea that there is often some interaction between instinct and learning can be found in experimental studies involving the production of danger signals between birds. Birds will alert each other with warning sounds to the presence of a possible predator. The production and reception of such sounds are regarded as innate, but in laboratory set-ups, an element of adaptation and learning has been discovered. This has been done by exposing birds to the alarm signal from another bird when in the presence of a neutral object rather than in the presence of a predatory animal. The neutral object might be something no more threatening than an empty bottle of washing-up liquid! In this manner birds can be taught to be 'frightened' of harmless objects. This, then, is a clear example of associative learning (through classical conditioning) combined with instinct.

Thinking

If an animal's goal-directed behaviour could truly be said to involve thinking and planning, then what are the requirements to classify it that way? Well, if the animal's problem-solving behaviour would appear to be the result of something more than experience through learning, imitation or trial-and-error (the nurture side of the argument) and something other than pre-programmed instinct (nature), then it could be argued that the animal was using thinking in order to achieve its goals. It could be argued that it is through the ability to think that humans have the feeling of free will, or at least the freedom from responding in a purely instinctive manner or behaving as a result of conditioning.

Early indications that **infra-human** species could achieve goals and solve problems by thinking things through before actually doing anything came from Köhler (1925). He observed that chimps appeared to display what might be regarded as insight. The animals seemed to produce novel and original solutions to problems. For example, they managed to get hold of bananas that were out of reach by joining sticks together that were lying around the cage. They could drag a box underneath some fruit placed just out of reach in order to stand on top of it to get at the food. Impressive though this sudden insight might at first appear, Köhler's observations were criticised because the chimps' previous history in the wild was unknown. Hence it could be argued that they had already learned by trial-and-error in the wild to achieve these kinds of solutions to such problems.

Implications for health

The nature–nurture debate is of central concern to those professionals working within both general and psychiatric medicine. For example, the main proposal of a recent study (Lichtenstein, 2000) is that environment rather than genetic make-up is the main determining factor in the development of the majority of cancers. This research, based upon the medical histories of more than 89,000 sets of twins, showed the relative contribution of genetic factors and environmental factors, such as general lifestyle, diet, smoking, etc. Comparison of identical – **monozygotic** – and non-identical – **dizygotic** – twins is regarded as being an almost ideal way of examining the nature–nurture debate. Identical twins have the exact same genes whereas non-identical twins do not. Lichtenstein's study asserts that all cancers are fundamentally genetic because they are 'triggered' by DNA defects that provoke the development of cancerous cells. Whereas susceptibility to various forms of cancer is genetically determined, it is exposure to different environmental factors and an individual's behaviour – such as smoking, drinking, lack of exercise, etc. – that ultimately decide whether or not a cancer actually develops. This study reports on a relatively low correspondence across sets of twins of the development of particular cancers. Its results indicate that the development of cancer dictated by nature was avoidable through appropriate nurturing.

Implications for psychiatry

In psychiatry, the nature–nurture debate has often focused upon schizophrenia. As with the above example, concerning the development of cancers, the nature side of the argument would stress that schizophrenia must be genetic in origin. However, the actual development of this condition might similarly be triggered by environmental factors. In fact the **diathesis-stress** approach proposes that avoidance of stress in daily life might serve to prevent the eventual triggering of schizophrenia. If this is indeed the case, then the sensible approach to tackling this devastating disorder would ideally be to identify the genetic marker for schizophrenia. That established, then individuals could be screened and potential sufferers could be advised and assisted in trying to avoid extreme sources of stress in their lives.

An historical perspective on the nature–nurture debate within psychiatry must focus upon the fact that the discussion has often been 'hijacked' for political ends. The works of R. D. Laing, the so-called 'anti-psychiatrist', stressed environmental factors in the aetiology, or origin, of schizophrenia. His writing was particularly political in nature because he proposed that mental illness was socially constructed. In short, he saw the dealings between psychiatrist and patient as something of a ritual whereby patients' distress was made worse because they were typically subjected to a 'culturing out' of any thoughts, feelings and behaviours that society might generally find unacceptable:

> ... psychiatry can so easily be a technique of brainwashing, of inducing behaviour that is adjusted ... In the best places, where straightjackets are abolished, doors are unlocked, leucotomies largely foregone, these can be replaced by more subtle lobotomies and tranquillizers that place the bars of Bedlam and the doors locked inside the patient. Thus I would wish to emphasise that our 'normal' 'adjusted' state is too often the abdication of ecstasy, the betrayal of our true potentialities ... (Laing, 1967, p. 12)

Schizophrenia: studies into the effects of the family environment

Thus environmental, rather than genetic, factors were highlighted as being central to what we call mental illness. Firstly, Laing insists in the above quote and elsewhere in his writing (e.g. *The Politics of Experience*) that concepts of normality are socially constructed in the first place. Secondly, he would argue that the micro-environment of the schizophrenic's family might be responsible for the patient's condition. *Sanity, Madness and the Family* (1970) presents reports on interviews with the immediate families of 11 schizophrenics. These present the families as 'schizogenic'. That is to say that the individual's 'schizophrenia' is an understandable reaction to or way of coping with the 'crazy' things going on in their immediate family. In line with this argument that madness made sense if viewed from the patient's point of view, Laing set about in *The Divided Self* (1959) to make sense – rather than nonsense – of the things said and done by his schizophrenic patients. However, present-day psychiatry cannot really be said to take Laing's rather extreme environmentalist claims too seriously. There was no control group of 'healthy' families to see whether or not disturbing things actually went on in all families, so whether anything was actually proven here is debatable. Additionally, twin studies (e.g. Shields, 1978) tend to support the genetic link for schizophrenia. Concordance rates, where both twins develop the disorder, for mono-zygotic twins are high and are, as the biological argument would predict, lower for dizygotic twins. There is the obvious criticism of such studies that the environment (including *in utero* conditions) of twins is similar, hence the nurture element could be an important factor.

Is stuttering innate?

Obviously the nature–nurture debate within psychiatry is not confined to schizophrenia. For example, why does stuttering develop in a very small minority of people whereas the rest of the population is not affected? It has often been proposed that psychological factors rather than brain abnormality might determine this affliction. However, recently some birds have been discovered that seem to produce a non-human version of stuttering (Rosenfield, 2000). A small minority of zebra finches have been found to repeat or get stuck on sub-units of normal song patterns. This evidence would tend to point to possible brain abnormality as the underlying cause. As with assessing the aetiology of schizophrenia, it should again be clear that actually teasing out the separate contributions of nature and nurture is a complex matter. Should brain abnormality be found in 'stuttering' finches, the question would still need to be addressed as to whether this abnormality is itself genetic in origin or in some way caused by some as yet unknown environmental factor.

Intelligence

Twin studies

As with the nature–nurture debate concerning schizophrenia, a comparison of monozygotic and dizygotic twins would appear to be an obvious method of teasing out the relative contribution made by genetic and environmental factors when looking at the intelligence of individuals. If the nature argument is to be followed, the correlation between IQ scores for sets of identical twins should be higher than for sets of non-identical twins. Similarly, if the nurture argument is to be followed, there should be lower correlations between the scores for sets of identical twins reared apart, and thus developing within a different environment, as opposed to identical twins reared together in the same environment. In fact twin studies tend to indicate the importance of both heredity and environment. However, such studies do raise methodological questions. What is actually similar about the environment of twins living together? How can we be certain that both individuals are treated identically, have the same experiences, etc.? Is it even possible to talk about *identical* environments? Simply pointing out that both twins are living under the same roof might be regarded as being just about as relevant as pointing out that they are both approximately 90 million miles away from the sun. That is to say that the 'sameness' that is being underlined is not necessarily an important or appropriate one. Methodological criticism can similarly be made of studies which claim to be looking at twins raised in different environments, because this ignores the important fact that they shared the same womb for nine months.

Imagine that you are writing the script for a science fiction film. This film concerns the perfect experiment for testing the nature–nurture debate regarding the issue of intelligence. Given that this is only fiction, and given that you have complete freedom to design any experiment of your choice, how would your film script tackle this question? Explain exactly how this perfect experiment would be carried out in the story-line of your film.

Progress exercise

The race and intelligence question

It is not unusual to find differences in average IQ test scores between identifiable groups within a population. For example, most American psychometric textbooks (e.g. Gregory, 1996; Kaplan and Saccuzzo, 1999) cite an average difference between African Americans and white Americans of approximately one **standard deviation**. Such a difference would mean that only about 16 per cent of the lower-scoring group would actually score above the mean of the higher group. Now, at first sight this might seem to be a strong argument for the nature side of the debate, but there are environmental complexities which need to be considered. If such tests were used for selection purposes for employment, then there is clearly the potential for adverse impact upon the lower-scoring group. Quite simply, there would be a systematic rejection of a significantly higher proportion of this group. This would result in lower salaries for this group which, in turn, would negatively affect the group's material wealth. This, needless to add, would determine the quality of the material environment within which this group would live. Well, if it is true that nurture, the environment, plays a role in eventual IQ, then the circular argument is clear in this set-up. There is a predictable pattern whereby the high-scoring group is continuously enriched in environmental terms, and if environment does matter, then this group is obviously advantaged. A self-fulfilling system at the sociological level; rather than what simplistically might have appeared to be the genetic level.

Perception

Efforts to find the interaction between naturally-occurring perceptual abilities and the effects that the environment can have upon them, include cross-cultural studies and investigations into the visual abilities of human infants and animals. Investigating the visual world of infants presents methodological difficulties in that the researcher obviously has to infer what the child is seeing or perceiving. Techniques for doing this include monitoring the child's normal, or baseline, sucking rate on a dummy. When presented with a novel, visual stimulus, the child's rate of sucking tends to change, either becoming more rapid or slower, so it can be inferred that the child has actually noticed some difference in the visual scene. In other words, the child can differentiate between stimuli. *Classical conditioning* has also been employed with infants and animals. This involves the repeated pairing of a particular visual stimulus with something which produces a reflex response. For instance, the infant or animal could be subjected to this repeated pairing. For example, the particular stimulus could be a large, coloured geometric shape such as a red triangle. This stimulus would be presented to the infant or animal. At the very same time as this is presented, something which produces a reflex response is also presented to the infant or animal. For example, a puff of air blown into the infant's or the animal's eye can be used to produce reflex blinking. This procedure is repeated until the visual stimulus alone produces the reflex response. If this conditioned reflex response is absent when a somewhat different stimulus is presented (such as a somewhat smaller red triangle), then it can be inferred that the child or animal can differentiate between the two stimuli. Size constancy in primates has been studied in this way. Visual illusions also give us some clue to the effects of learning and experience on perception. Illusions and a phenomenon referred to as 'blindsight' will be explained in the next sections, followed by some comments on studies with animals.

Visual illusions

There are many well-known visual illusions that provide us with insights into how perception works. With reference to the ambiguous figure below (Figure 6.1), where it is possible to perceive either a vase or the profile of two human faces, Miller speculates: 'So it might happen in a Martian world where in fact they'd never seen a species that had profiles of that sort, but where they were accomplished vase makers, that they wouldn't understand why we thought of this as an illusion at all. They would see only vases' (1983, p. 51).

In terms of the nature–nurture debate, it should be evident from this illustration that the environment seems to be responsible for 'tuning' the visual system into perceiving things in a particular way. Miller naturally suspects that because a Martian might well inhabit an

Figure 6.1 **An ambiguous figure**

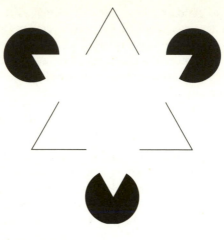

Figure 6.2 **Kanizsa's triangle**

environment without human-like faces, then the perceptual system would not regard this as being ambiguous at all.

Similarly Figure 6.2 is unlikely to be perceived as the disparate collection of elements of which it is actually comprised. Rather than interpreting these miscellaneous pieces of visual data as such, it is almost impossible not to perceive this as three black circles and two triangles. As with Miller's speculation above as to how a Martian might perceive Figure 6.1, here it could be proposed that should a culture exist where geometric configurations such as circles and triangles simply do not exist, then it would be precisely this odd collection of elements that would in fact be seen. Along similar lines, it has been suggested that the lesser degree of susceptibility to the Müller-Lyer (Figure 6.3) illusion that has been found amongst people in some parts of the world is due to the fact that they live in less 'carpentered' environments. Again, the argument underlines the importance of the environment and past visual experience. Figure 6.4 is usually read incorrectly as 'Paris in the Spring'. This is quite simply because experience has taught us that sentences usually make good sense. Hence, the reader naturally tends to 'edit out' the repeated word 'the'.

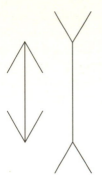

Figure 6.3 **Müller–Lyer illusion**

Figure 6.4 **The influence of expectations based upon past experience. What does this well-known sentence actually say?**

Studies with humans

Weiskrantz's blindsight studies (1986) clearly indicated that biological damage to the visual cortex, for example through injury or stroke, results in the individual being unable to consciously acknowledge visual stimuli within certain areas of the visual field, although s/he is typically able to behave as if s/he is processing the information elsewhere in the brain. Hence the name of the phenomenon, 'blindsight'. Moreover it is known that damage to the more primitive areas of the visual system that terminate in the mid-brain can result in a phenomenon which has been termed 'visual neglect'. Here the individual reports that visual stimuli are consciously seen; however, such stimuli are often ignored or neglected as if they were not of importance. For survival purposes any healthy animal will attend and react to stimuli which present themselves in the environment. The above clinical cases concerning 'blindsight' and 'visual neglect' underline the importance of the nature

121

side of the nature–nurture debate relating to perception, because an animal requires an intact visual system for normal functioning to develop. Weiskrantz's patients had their particular visual problems as a direct result of the fact that their visual system was not fully intact.

However, for normal visual perception to develop in any animal the nurture side of the equation must also be in place. The following section outlines experimental manipulation of the visual environment of animals in order to tease out the effects of the nurture side of the equation.

Studies with animals

Weiskrantz studied human subjects with accidental damage to the visual system. Interventions in the quality of the visual environment, in order to distinguish the effects of nurture from nature, have usually involved animals. Blakemore and Cooper (1970), for example, illustrated that a properly functioning visual system must be the result of an interaction between nature and nurture. It is simply not enough to have a healthy, intact visual system. The environment must also be healthy. Ideally it should be rich and stimulating promoting and nurturing full development of what nature has provided. To illustrate this, kittens were placed by Blakemore and Cooper into an environment that failed to nurture full and healthy development of perceptual capacities. The kittens were reared from birth in complete darkness except for several hours each day when some of the kittens were placed inside drums painted with vertical stripes. The researchers discovered that this lack of stimulation – or nurture – resulted in apparent 'blindness' to those stimuli subsequently presented to the kittens that were horizontally orientated, although the kittens reacted normally to vertically orientated stimuli. A second group of kittens, exposed only to horizontal lines, seemed 'blind' to vertically presented stimuli. In addition, the researchers found that examination of the cells in the animals' visual cortices through the use of microelectrodes failed to discover cells that fired in response to horizontally or vertically presented bars of light respectively for the two groups of kittens. As with Miller's Martian mentioned in the 'Visual illusions' section, the environment (nurture) again has effects upon what nature has bestowed. This research by Blakemore and Cooper is described more fully in the *Study aids* section, Chapter Eight.

Summary

This chapter dealt with a fundamental debate in psychology that touches on several different topic areas. Those examined included perception, intelligence, psychiatry, and the relationship between language and thought. Developmental psychology is also inevitably a part of this debate because it is concerned with examining, amongst other things, the 'normal' psychological stages that children pass through as they mature. The psychologist Piaget, for example, proposed that these stages are determined by the 'nature' part of the equation in that all children go through particular developmental stages in the same order and roughly at the same age. There is of course the environmental side of the argument to consider. And thus developmental psychologists are also interested in examining ways in which improved environments (nurture) can maximise the child's potential and psychological development.

Further reading

Gregory, R. L. (1966) *Eye and Brain*, London: Weidenfeld & Nicolson. A popular text which provides useful additional material with respect to innate and learned aspects of visual pereption.

Laing, R. D. (1965) *The Politics of Experience and the Bird of Paradise*, London: Penguin [1990].

Laing, R. D. and Esterson, A. (1970) *Sanity, Madness and the Family*, London: Penguin [1990]. This text presents 11 case studies concerning the family environment of schizophrenics. Here Laing and his co-writers attempt to establish the argument that it is the environment, rather than biological or genetic factors, that causes some individuals to develop schizophrenic symptoms.

Gross, R. D. (1995) *Themes, Issues & Debates in Psychology*, London: Hodder & Stoughton. Chapter 5: 'Heredity and environment' is a clearly written text suitable for the A-level candidate.

7

Behaviourism

Behaviourism and psychology

Psychology is often described as the study of mental processes, or the mind, and behaviour. Indeed many general texts in psychology are often deliberately sub-titled in such a manner as to highlight the full scope of the discipline. Mental processes, however, are less readily observable than openly available behaviour. Mental processes are private events. Although, we usually avoid the use of terms such as 'events' when talking about activities that go on in our heads. At the biological level, these might be termed 'physiological processes'. At the level of private awareness, these might be termed 'experiences'. Public events are things that happen within the physical world, but which can be observed by others. The activities of the mind, however, are private. As such, they can only be examined by the person experiencing these activities. Of course, they can be reported to another person, but these introspective reports are not always reliable or accurate. (For instance, refer to the example concerning hypnosis in Chapter Two.)

Private experience and public behaviour

When reading this psychology text you privately experience a number of different things. These might include impatience, 'why doesn't this writer just get to the point?'; confusion, 'what is written here seems to be contradicted by the previous sentence'; annoyance, 'what I'm reading now seems quite irrelevant to assisting me in passing my examination'; or perhaps enlightenment, 'Yes. Now I see what this is leading to.'

So much for that which might be experienced in private. But all that would be evident to others while you read this text would be your behaviour whist reading. This brings us to a philosophical issue to be discussed at some length later in this chapter, referred to as the 'problem of other minds'.

Judging a person's private experience from their public behaviour

Now suppose another person was observing the reader. What could they know of the reader's thoughts and private experiences? The answer to this depends on what the reader's behaviour is likely to be. I would only be able to judge what the reader was experiencing by looking at his/her behaviour. Such behaviour might include smiling, nodding, grimacing, shaking and scratching the head, or throwing the text on the fire. The point here is that I can only *infer* that such behaviours are indices of your experience. Such behaviour may point to a range of emotions and experiences. But another individual, an objective observer, would never be certain that such inferences were correct. Your throwing the book on the fire might be due to something like disgust, but it might also, although it's rather unlikely, be an indication that the reader was feeling cold and needed to boost the output of the fire somewhat. Or it might indicate that the reader was suffering from some form of mental illness. Equally, things other than failing to understand what s/he is reading can cause a person to scratch their head, such as an itchy head. In short, there would always be an element of doubt, and for the strict behaviourist, such an element of doubt is avoidable and hence should be avoided. For the behaviourist, only observable, and therefore publicly available, behaviours are the legitimate data for analysis.

As an approach to psychology then, behaviourism was a sincere attempt to bring the discipline out of the domain of private experience and into the public arena of scientific scrutiny. The method of 'introspection' as practised by Wundt during the last quarter of the nineteenth century relied on a technique which involved 'looking in' on one's own private conscious mental processes. This looking in on private experience was an attempt to analyse that which was consciously experienced into its constituent, or basic, elements. However, behaviourists would argue that only that which could be objectively observed, by several observers at the same time, should be included in the psychologist's endeavours. Anything else was in danger of being merely speculative and potentially untrue.

Knowing

This emphasis on observable behaviour was a clear attempt to eliminate speculation. This approach is very clearly linked with the idea of not only knowing; but also of knowing that what is known is 'true'. Referring back to the above illustration, I can know that the reader of the text scratched their head. I clearly know this to be the case, but I can only *infer* that this might be an indication of confusion. Head scratching is an observable behaviour, it is measurable, and it is easier to measure, record and report upon than are unobservable and private mental states. It was from this standpoint concerning knowledge that behaviourism came to dominate psychology for much of the twentieth century. Psychologists had to know that their data was obtained in a scientific way. Only in this manner could psychology align itself to the pure sciences. With the technological advances in the last century that have resulted from the success of 'hard' science, it is no surprise that psychology should try to emulate its objective stance, and in so doing, reject the introspective method.

The philosophical problems associated with the doing of science, and in particular concerning the way in which knowledge about the world is obtained and accounted for, are referred to as 'epistemological' concerns – the extent to which the scientist is convinced that what is known about the world is actually true. Speculation and unreasonable indirect inferences were seen by the behaviourist as being unnecessary. Mental states are not directly knowable or observable by another individual, and so, claimed behaviourists, they were not necessary – or even desirable – and thus need not be brought to the attention of any psychologist wishing to be sure of establishing psychology as a 'correctly' formulated discipline.

Behaviourism as a theoretical approach to psychology

What is a theory? How does theory help with scientific enquiry?

Theory can be defined as being something that is postulated or suggested in order to attempt to explain things that have already been observed. Thus it tries to provide a unifying explanation. Theory can also assist in guiding the scientist's future observations, and then to help the scientist to explain such observations. Freud's theory of the unconscious, for example, served as an attempt to explain so-called **slips of the tongue**. It also provided an account of what might drive apparently irrational behaviour in terms of unconscious wishes to act in a self-destructive manner. With regard to the development of theoretical statements concerning behaviourism, several important observations of animals had been documented in academic journals. These included Thorndike (1911), Pavlov (1927), and later, Skinner (1938). These observations all had one thing in common – they all involved learning by association. These associations are outlined very briefly below, and it is these associations that underlie behaviourism's postulation of learning theory. *Theoretically* all behaviour can be accounted for in terms of associative learning, so behaviourism may be regarded as a 'theory' for psychology because not only does it propose an explanation to unify existing observations concerning behaviour, it also provided a framework within which future observations would be guided.

Thorndike's law of effect

In Thorndike's experiments the association learned by the animal involved its operating on its environment – behaviour – in order to achieve desired results – reward. An animal was put into a 'puzzle box' and, by trial-and-error, it would eventually escape in order to reach a food reward. Thorndike termed this the Law of effect. According to this law, what happens as a result of behaviour will influence the likelihood of that behaviour being repeated in the future. As noted above, this kind of learning involves the idea of trial-and-error, and importantly it should be stressed that no 'thinking' need be involved. Behaviour that leads to pleasant consequences tends to become 'stamped in', and behaviour leading to unpleasant consequences tends to disappear, or to become 'stamped out'. In everyday conversation we call this 'reward' and 'punishment' respectively.

Skinner

Skinner's observations involved the 'Skinner box', where rats would be observed pressing levers, or, in the case of pigeons, pecking at keys, in order to obtain food rewards. The behavioural tendency of the rats to press the lever becomes more frequent because of the reward associated with it. That is to say, the behaviour is strengthened by 'positive reinforcement'. The rats also learn to press levers in order to avoid unpleasant consequences, such as electric shocks. This latter state of affairs would be referred to as 'negative reinforcement'. Here the animal exhibits behaviour with the result that it avoids unpleasant consequences. Note that there is an important difference here between 'negative reinforcement' and 'punishment'. The former actually requires particular behaviour to be exhibited for the animal to avoid unpleasant consequences – in other words, particular behaviour is 'stamped in' – the latter simply refers to the elimination – or the 'stamping out' – of particular behaviour because of the unpleasant consequences that are associated with that behaviour. An example of this would be that a parent smacking a small child is likely to provide an unpleasant association that will tend to eliminate the undesired behaviour that the child was exhibiting at the time that it was smacked. But the child does not learn what it might be that the parent actually wishes the child to do instead. The important point here is that the organism makes associations between behaviour and its results.

Pavlov's classical conditioning

It should be noted that the above accounts concerned the animal actively operating on its environment. For this reason the term 'operant conditioning' is often employed to describe this type of learning. A rather more basic and passive type of learning relates to the association or pairing of stimuli and reflex responses. Pavlov noted that a previously neutral stimulus for eliciting salivation, i.e. the sound of a bell, could, through being presented alongside the 'unconditioned stimulus' of food, acquire the status of becoming a 'conditioned stimulus' which would later produce salivation on its own. Hungry dogs naturally, unconditionally, salivate when food is presented. That is why the food is referred to as the 'unconditioned stimulus'. Pavlov was able to condition the dogs by repeatedly presenting food to the hungry animals and, at the same time, ringing a bell. The dogs would thus learn – associate – the sound of the bell with the food. Pavlov found that eventually this association was so successfully formed that the dogs would then salivate merely at the sound of the bell. Thus, the sound of the bell became the conditioned stimulus.

Conclusion

The above accounts all underline the importance of associations between behaviour and events in the animal's or person's environment. The theory concluded from these observations is as follows: all behaviour, animal and human alike, can be explained in terms of learning. That is to say, everything we know and all the behaviours, complex or otherwise, that we exhibit are the result of experience. This proposition presented a potentially huge task for the behaviourist, but it also proposed a paradigm for psychology – an all-embracing framework within which it was going to be possible for psychologists to account for all human behaviour. This led to Watson's famous claim for providing this full account.

> Give me a dozen healthy infants, well-formed, and my own specified world to bring them up in and I'll guarantee to take one at random and train him to become any type of specialist I might select . . . doctor, lawyer, artist, merchant-chief and, yes, even beggar-man and thief, regardless of his talents, penchants,

tendencies, abilities, vocations, and race of his ancestors. (Watson 1924, p. 104)

This was a brave, if rather arrogant, claim. As a practical venture Watson's proposed project would be colossal and as such quite unmanageable. However, this claim is really a theoretical stance only, rather than a serious research proposal. Nevertheless, what it does provoke is speculation that should an individual child in the real world grow up to be a beggarman, or indeed a highly respected doctor, to what extent is this the product of externally determined, environmental, factors?

For behaviourism, of course, environment is all. For the behaviourist, it is through the associations of reward and punishment that an individual is formed. This kind of environmental determinism, then, would suggest that the highly respected doctor would come to be so because of rewards set up in the environment. These would include financial rewards, referred to in the behaviourist account as 'secondary reinforcers', and social reinforcement, praise and encouragement from parents, friends, etc., and so on. Watson, of course, was insisting that all that was needed was control over the environment in order to 'shape' the child.

On the other hand, you might speculate concerning the helpless and needy beggarman, unable to get himself sorted out sufficiently to hold down any career or job. Presumably the behaviourist would regard this individual as being a victim of what Seligman described as **learned helplessness**. There are two major problems with Watson's claim. Firstly, the idea that it is the environment only that shapes the individual leads to the abolition of notions of right or wrong. For how can a person be held responsible for what they have become? How can they be seen as being to 'blame' for what they have done or failed to do? If Watson's claim that external factors in the environment determine and 'shape' behaviour, does this not take control away from the individual and make the environment the deciding or controlling factor? This 'environmental determinism' surely robs the individual of freedom and of responsibility. (The freedom–responsibility question is dealt with more fully in Chapter Two.) The second problem involves the difficult shift from theory to practical science.

Behaviourism as a theory and as a practical venture

The kind of determinism proposed by Watson works well 'backwards', so to speak. It is relatively easy to claim from a behavioural-determinist stance that the end-product, for example, the doctor mentioned previously, is the result of environmental conditioning, but this conditioning is now hidden in the doctor's past and experience: it is not available for scrutiny. The behaviourist's reply to this would be that although this is the case, practical problems still do not upset the theoretical foundations on which Watson's claim is made. Anyway, these practical problems are not unique to psychology. Imagine the folly inherent in posing the following question to a so-called 'pure scientist'.

> You tell me that you know much concerning the laws of nature. How materials bend, break, melt. You know all about the laws of aerodynamics. How things float on the air or plummet to the ground. If this indeed is so, please tell me then where that particular leaf on that particular tree is going to fall in autumn?

The scientist's reply to the above would have to be that this kind of question is on such a huge scale that it is impossible to make that kind of prediction. There are too many variables acting upon each other for it to be possible to plot their effects all at once. The leaf's eventual path in autumn might appear to be subject to the random forces of chaos, but this does not mean for one moment that the leaf ever stops obeying the laws of nature that we know to be true, nor that its path is also determined by external environmental forces.

It is for these reasons that behaviourism established its laws within the deliberately limited 'sub-world' of the laboratory. For example, in operant conditioning the lawful relationship between various *schedules of reinforcement* and the subsequent resistance to extinction was established. In other words, the laws of behaviour were discovered within relatively small and controlled environments, not within the 'real world'. However, this is not to say that such laws, once established, do not also operate in the world outside of the laboratory. Quite on the contrary, behaviourism has been extensively applied in 'real life'. Indeed several applications are actually outlined in the sections below where behaviourism is scrutinised in terms of its positive and negative aspects.

Behaviourism and private experience

For private mental states to be put to one side because they are outside of the scope of scientific enquiry is legitimate enough. Similarly legitimate is behaviourism's exclusion of mentalistic discourse (language) from the discipline. Words like thinking, hoping, expecting and wishing are inappropriate because they relate to private, inner states and are therefore outside of behaviourism's insistence that the only valid data for psychology should be observable behaviour. The term 'data', of course, is taken from the Latin word meaning 'given things'. It is easy to see why exhibited behaviour is a given thing, because it can be observed, received, by any observer. Thoughts, hopes, expectations, desires and wishes are not given things as such, for they relate to personal inner conditions and cannot be directly *given* (or made available) to others. For example, I cannot directly observe, measure or record your hopes, fears, delight or boredom; however, I can infer such things from your behaviour.

A student may be experiencing interest in a class, but that interest belongs to the student. The student can only provide, or 'give away', behaviour which is indicative of interest. Such behaviour is not too difficult to spot and may include looking at the teacher, nodding, or even verbal behaviour – for example by uttering particular words usually associated with what we call 'interest'. For the strict behaviourist, though, this would simply be verbal behaviour which may or may not be indicative of an inner state of genuine interest. There would still be an element of doubt. Indeed, it would be this element of doubt which would exclude such inferences from the behaviourist's account. The available data would be, for example, that the student uttered a quantifiable number of words. That is to say that a certain amount of verbal behaviour was 'exhibited'.

Practical implications: the clinical setting

Imagine that you are writing a novel and that you wish to describe a person suffering from depression. Write a short account of your depressed character. Now read the following.

Progress exercise

Depression

It is no surprise that whenever behaviourism has been applied in the clinical setting, there has been a tendency to avoid mentalistic discourse. That is, to avoid using words that relate to the patient's private experience. Thus a patient may be called 'depressed', but only because this is inferred by the behaviour exhibited, or, rather, the tendency for the patient not to show much behaviour at all. In this case, the lack of exhibited behaviour would be seen as an indication of depression. There would be no need to call upon the patient's private experience. Consequently, the therapeutic goal is focused on the behaviour – or lack of it – rather than attempting to treat this elusive 'thing' that a person 'has' that is called 'depression'.

> **Progress exercise**
>
> Examine your account of a depressed person from the previous progress exercise. What can be said about your character's behaviour? Did your character exhibit many behaviours or few? What behaviours, if any were exhibited, were characteristic of depression? Did you refer to inner thoughts or feelings much? How does your account fit in with the way in which a behaviourist would account for depression? In what ways does your account differ?

Behaviourism and explanatory fictions: mental way-stations

In his attempt to rid psychology of unnecessary references to unobservable mental aspects, Skinner argued that the way in which we talk about human or animal learning and behaviour is crucial. In his view, it is pointless to invoke what he called **mental way-stations** in order to 'tell a good story' about why the organism behaves as it does in a particular case. Thus, when we state that the animal drinks water *because it is thirsty*, we are unhelpfully adding a private unobservable experience – feeling or being 'thirsty', a word that behaviourists do not allow, to what is already a satisfactory account. (That is, the measurement and observation of the animal's tendency or otherwise to drink water.)

So, behaviourists would argue that nobody *has* 'depression'. They certainly wouldn't introduce a mental way-station by suggesting that a person is in a depressed state of mind. Rather they would argue that instead of talking about having this thing called depression, we should simply define depression in behavioural terms. That is, depression should be defined as a tendency not to behave very much. As such, then, the logical step towards treating depression is to go straight to treating the absence of behaviour. In short, to setting up the necessary conditions of reward (and perhaps punishment) to ensure that the patient starts *behaving* again. Obviously the patient would be encouraged to start exhibiting desirable and positive behaviours such as getting out of bed, washing, taking exercise, etc.; not negative or harmful behaviours such as smoking. So-called **token economies** have often been employed in order to provide this type of treatment.

Rejection of mental way-stations: the law of parsimony

Similarly, Skinner would argue that the way in which we talk about how animals learn is entwined with the way in which we *choose* to account for this learning. Skinner, for example, would avoid reference to unobservable events beneath the animal's skin, so to speak. To include these would be unscientific, unnecessary and uneconomical. In the following short extract, Skinner argues that the inclusion of 'private' mental factors is totally unnecessary.

> Where an experimental analysis might examine the effect of punishment on behavior, a mentalistic psychology will be concerned first with the effect of punishment in generating feelings of anxiety and then with the effect of anxiety on behavior. The mental state seems to bridge the gap between dependent and independent variables . . . (Skinner, in Wann, 1964, p. 90)

Bridging this gap, then, between the punishment and its effect on behaviour allows the account to 'tell a good story'. By including this idea of 'generating feelings of anxiety' a more thorough account would seem to be provided. However, according to Skinner, such vague and unobservable intervening variables as this should be eliminated from an objective and scientific account.

The law of parsimony and 'explanatory fictions'

If there is an observable link between punishment and subsequent behaviour, there is no need to 'fill out' the account with unobservable, and therefore questionable, speculation about anxiety, etc. Avoiding such speculation would be in line with what is known as the **law of parsimony**. For example, if we can account for a person's excessive drinking without referring to non-observable concepts such as alcoholism, addiction, desire to drink, need to drink, and wish to self-destroy, then we should simply do so. If we define an alcoholic as someone who drinks too much alcohol, then that is fine as a definition. However, to attempt to explain someone's excessive drinking as because they are an alcoholic is a circular argument: an explanatory fiction.

The law of parsimony also extends to the way in which behaviourists view clinical treatment. Alcoholism, for example, has often been treated through classical conditioning. This procedure simply pairs an emetic with alcohol. An emetic is a substance that makes a person feel nauseous. This is an *unconditioned* stimulus for the vomiting (i.e. *unconditioned*) response. After several pairings of nausea and vomiting, the person being treated acquires a *conditioned response*, vomiting, to alcohol. The alcohol, of course, having acquired the status of *conditioned stimulus*. This treatment is known as aversion therapy.

In re-reading the above treatment of an alcoholic, it can be noted that nowhere in this account is there any mention of inner, unobservable mental way-stations, such as the patient comes to *fear* taking alcohol; has learned to *expect* to *feel* nauseous; *realises* that taking alcohol will . . . etc. Importantly, what must be noted is the exclusive concern with behavioural factors.

Anthropomorphism and mental way-stations

Anthropomorphism is the tendency to attribute human-like characteristics to animals. Similarly, the word *animism* is when objects are described as if they were human. The children's song 'The sun has got his hat on' is an example of talking about an object as if it were a person. The tendency to try to avoid reference to inner, mental states in the previous description of *aversion therapy* treatment for alcoholics complies with the way the strict behaviourist attempts to avoid such descriptions when conditioning 'lower' animals.

In the following quotation, Skinner discusses the tendency for his students to invoke the non-observable (and for the behaviourist 'outlawed') world of private experience. Here they fall into the trap of speculating upon the 'pigeon's private world':

> ... In a demonstration experiment, a hungry pigeon was conditioned to turn around in a clockwise direction. A final, smoothly executed pattern of behavior was shaped by reinforcing successive approximations with food. Students who had watched the demonstration were asked to write an account of what they had seen. Their responses included the following: (1) The organism was conditioned to **expect** reinforcement for the right kind of behavior. (2) The pigeon walked around, **hoping** that something would bring the food back again. (3) The pigeon **observed** that a certain behavior seemed to produce a particular result. (4) The pigeon **felt** that food would be given it because of its action; and (5) the bird came to **associate** his action with the click of the food dispenser. (Skinner in Wann, 1964, p. 91)

For Skinner, of course, the private inner world of expectations, hopes, feelings, etc. are all unnecessary mental way-stations between the food reward and its subsequent effects upon the pigeon's behaviour. For the strict behaviorist, then, such terms are superfluous even when accounting for human learning. What a crime, therefore, that his students should employ these terms for the pigeon. Not only are they guilty of calling upon mental way-stations, they have also fallen into the trap of anthropomorphism.

Eliminating mentalistic discourse

Behaviourists carefully avoid employing language that tends to relate to the unobservable inner life of an individual. Not only are words like hope, despair, expectation, thinking and feeling dispensed with but hunger and thirst could be replaced in behavioural terms. Thus, thirst could be replaced with 'tendency to drink', hunger with 'tendency to eat', and so on. Redundant too are terms such as inner drive, motivation or determination. For these too are, by definition, far too private. These need to be re-defined employing a rather more objective discourse. For example, Warden (1931) developed an experimental 'method of obstruction'.

In this set-up, white rats were placed in a simple environment consisting of two chambers which were separated by an electrified passageway. The hungry rat was placed in one chamber. In the other, food. Measuring the strength of the motivation (or hunger by another name) was quite simple and objective. The experimenter simply had to record the amount of time the rat would endure the electrified section in order to obtain the food. In fact, Warden observed that motivation was highest for a rat separated from her offspring. This was followed by thirst, hunger and sex. To the behaviourist, the unobservable discourse that talked of 'motivation', 'drive', and 'determination' could be replaced by an objective, observable and quantifiable account of what the animal actually did.

Behaviourism and the mind

Behavioural tendencies and dispositions

The observations recorded by Warden re-define words like 'drive' by introducing units of behaviour that can be measured (crossing an electrified grille, for example). It could be argued that a hungry rat has a tendency to behave in a particular way, for example, to cross an electrified grille repeatedly to get food. Whereas a rat that is not hungry would not cross it. The hungry rat is in a dispositional state to do so. This is, of course, an inner biological state, or condition, that drives or directs the rat towards food, or to eat.

Similarly, to say that glass is fragile is to imply that it is in a particular physical state, and this state is such that it tends to break into pieces if hit with a heavy object. Its fragility – like the rat's motivation or drive – is not a 'thing' that can be observed. Talking about its fragility is a way of talking about its tendency to behave in a certain manner if it is hit.

If we refer to someone as being 'bad-tempered', this is a way of talking about their tendency to behave in a particular way. This presumably implies that this person is in a particular physical state. That is to say that the person is in a particular brain state and/or hormonal state, and, presumably, a person in this state tends to feel in a bad mood, a direct subjective feeling of anger.

The problem here is that only our bad-tempered person can feel their own anger. I cannot experience (or observe) their anger. I can only experience my own inner state of serenity, or whatever it might be. Thus the bad-tempered person can be said to have direct access to, or immediate acquaintance with, this psychological (brain) state of anger, and only I can have this kind of acquaintance with my serenity.

Now I can certainly provoke or taunt this person in order to test the assumed predisposition towards anger. Although the evidence will be rather second-hand. I will infer by their foot-stamping and shouting that they are angry, but I can only know that they are angry in the weak sense of 'knowing'. The angry person knows that they are angry in the strong sense of 'knowing', for it is their anger. This weak knowledge that I have about another's experience is referred to as the *problem of other minds*.

The problem of other minds

If I cut myself, I know that I experience pain in a very real way. For I have strong conscious knowledge of my pain in the most direct way possible. But how do I know that another person is in pain if they cut themselves? Well, I know this in a weak sense, because I infer this from the other person's behaviour, but the other person may be a very good actor, and simply exhibiting the behaviours that I know I exhibit when in pain. It is easy to imagine that a robot could be programmed to exhibit such behaviour. Would we then say that the robot is 'in pain' just because its behaviour suggests this?

It is probably reasonable to admit that this philosophical problem is *unverifiable*. That is, there is no way of testing or indicating conclusively that another person is in pain.

Other minds and the argument from analogy

If I propose that other people are conscious, have thoughts and feelings, feel pain, and so on, this proposal is based upon an *analogy* that I am making with myself. Analogous logic, of course, is a form of reasoning that states that if two things are similar in some respects, then they are likely to be similar in other respects. So, if my behaviour when in pain is to scream, shout, wince, etc., and, if other people behave likewise when they are in situations similar to those in which I know myself to be in pain, then because other people are like me in so many respects, I am driven by this comparison – or analogy – to conclude that the other person is in pain.

Strictly speaking any argument that is based on only one case is not very convincing. Here, of course, the only case with which the comparison is made is myself. Hospers (1990) outlines why such an argument is so frail:

> Suppose I see a set of boxes stored in someone's garage. I open one box and find that it is full of books. I do not open any of the rest, but I say, "Since all the boxes look pretty much alike, I infer that they all contain books." Admittedly this wouldn't be a very safe inference, and you wouldn't bet much on it. The boxes might contain anything – trinkets, papers, children's toys. If you open only one box, you're not in a very good position to say that they all contain books. Your position would be much better if you had opened all the boxes but one, found that they contained books, and then inferred that probably the last box would contain books also. . . . But is not that exactly the position we are in with regard to other minds? In my own case, I have (1) my behaviour and (2) my feeling pain. But in every other case, I have only the behavior to go by. So am I not in the position of the person who concludes that all the boxes contain books, on the slender basis of finding that one box contains books? (Hospers, 1990, p. 251)

The problem of other minds for all practical purposes

This problem is probably the kind that can never really be resolved. It is rather similar to asking someone whether or not they always tell the truth. How convincing is their answer ever going to be? They may say that they always tell the truth, but this could really be one of those occasions when they are telling a lie, and I have only their verbal behaviour to go on. I cannot know (as the other person will know in a direct manner, or 'at first hand', so to speak) whether or not they are telling a lie. I can only infer whether or nor a lie is being told at one remove or in an indirect manner.

Similarly, another person's behaviour, verbal or otherwise, is never going to resolve my problem in knowing whether or not they have thoughts, feelings, experiences of pain, etc. For all practical purposes, however, most people do actually go around assuming that others have minds, experience pain, and so on.

Imagine a dreadful situation in which a young child dies. In such circumstances, no one would suggest that anyone really goes through a formal philosophical inner debate about whether the tears of the child's mother are mere behaviour. Surely we would normally draw the conclusion that she is indeed in an emotional/mental state of grief. Another person, of course, cannot experience *her* grief. Although we can certainly experience other emotions ourselves, such as deep pity, as a result of witnessing her behaviour. That is, behaviour indicative of her inner torment. At times like this it is wise, even for the most rigorous behaviourist, to put to one side this radical refusal to accept the existence of other minds. In this case, the most normal and healthy reaction to the sight of the mother is to accept your beliefs about her state of mind at that particular moment in time.

Again, for all practical purposes, medical professionals put aside the problem of other minds when they administer anaesthetic to a badly injured, yet paralysed, patient. Being paralysed might dictate that no behaviour usually associated with pain is actually exhibited. Surely it would be madness for a surgeon to engage in clever philosophical debate concerning the problem of other minds when really s/he should get on with the business of alleviating the pain in the patient. Indeed should a surgeon fail to put aside the problem of other minds, this would legally be regarded as a neglect of professional duties. The fact that the surgeon only has a weak knowledge of the patient's pain becomes something of an irrelevance when faced with the practical circumstances with which s/he is faced.

Other minds and artificial intelligence

A question that has been repeatedly posed by those psychologists working in machine intelligence is 'can machines think?'. Moreover, this question has probably been set in so many examination papers for students studying psychology at university that it has become something of a cliché.

Imagine yourself playing chess against a machine. (And small chess-playing machines do play very good chess.) After you have made your move, there will be some delay before the machine makes its move. During this delay the computer is programmed to re-evaluate the state of play, and then to make the best move possible. So, what is happening in between your move and the computer's? Is the computer thinking? It would certainly seem to be doing so. Because, after all, it *behaves* as if it is doing something like thinking. Its behaviour is not random. In fact it is very intelligent, and such machines win a lot of games of chess.

Well, of course it is thinking. But that does rather depend upon how you define the thinking. If your definition is 'whatever goes on inside the machine in between my move and its move', then it is thinking.

But the situation here is obviously linked to the problem of other minds. All you have direct access to is the machine's behaviour, and it is from this that you can infer that 'thinking', as defined, is taking place. Again that word 'infer'. What you know for certain is that it has behaved in a particular manner. You cannot know for certain that anything like thinking (again, as defined) is going on.

Review exercise

(a) Reflect on the chapter that you have just read and draw up a list of all the connections that you can think of between this chapter and the other debates and issues covered elsewhere in this text, then add an explanatory sentence after each connection that you have listed. For example, 'behaviourism is a reductionist approach'. Here you might make a note as to just why and in what way this can be described as such. Similarly, 'behaviourism provides a strong case for the nurture side of the nature–nurture debate'. Make brief notes as to why this can be said to be the case. (b) Now draw up a list of connections between other chapters. For example, how do various positions on the mind–body problem (Chapter Four) relate to issues concerning free will (Chapter Two)? This exercise will hopefully help you to build up ideas for illustrating your answers to examination questions. Remember that, whilst answering the set question, a good essay will show an awareness as to how the debates actually relate to each other.

Summary

The review exercise above points to the reason why this text ends with a chapter covering behaviourism. For behaviourism does tend to apply to the major debates covered in this part of the A-level syllabus. In the examination you may feel it appropriate to illustrate an answer to a question on a particular debate in psychology by drawing upon material presented in this chapter. Here are a few examples.

Debate: free will and determinism

An examination question concerning the issue of free will could be answered with some reference to behaviourism. Behaviourists propose that *all* behaviour is the result of learning. As we have seen, Watson went so far as to claim (pp. 130–131) that he could 'produce' any kind of individual – artist, lawyer or thief – if only he could have control over that individual's environment. If such a claim is to be taken seriously, then the very idea of free will would become nonsensical.

Debate: reductionism

Reductionist approaches have been examined in Chapter Three. Such approaches included biological reductionism and the evolutionary perspective. Behaviourism is another example of the reductionist approach. By studying comparatively simple animals such as rats and pigeons and by studying them in a relatively simple environment, such as the 'Skinner Box', behaviourists were able to identify the principles involved when learning takes place. Behaviourists would argue that complex behaviour in humans is actually composed of many simple units of associative learning; thus, what appears to be complex can be reduced down to its more basic components.

Debate: can psychology be a science?

If a question asks you to consider whether or not psychology could be a science, then you could argue that psychology indeed could have been a science if behaviourism had been accepted as the agreed way of investigation and research in psychology. The idea of an 'agreed way' of proceeding is often referred to as a scientific paradigm. But behaviourism was *not* accepted as a paradigm, and it was not accepted for the variety of reasons presented in this chapter. In preparation for the examination, you may wish to make a list of what these reasons were by re-reading this chapter. One reason is that behaviourism insisted that the 'proper' subject matter for psychology should only be observable behaviour. Behaviourists would argue that restricting the subject matter to observable behaviour only would allow psychology to proceed along 'scientific' lines. This was a reasonable argument apart from the fact that it would eliminate anything to do with mental life from psychology. Surely mental life must be investigated unless you change the definition of psychology to exclude anything to do with the 'mind'?

Debate: nature–nurture

As has been mentioned in several places above, behaviourists were very much concerned with controlling the environment in order to shape an animal's behaviour. For the behaviourist, the nurture side of the debate was of utmost importance.

Further reading

Jarvis, M. (2000) *Theoretical Approaches in Psychology*, London: Routledge. Chapter 2: 'Behavioural psychology'. This provides good supportive material on the topic of behaviourism and is also in the Routledge Modular Series. It is interesting and helpful to get another author's approach.

Hunt, M. (1993) *The Story of Psychology*, London: Anchor Books. Chapter 9: 'The behaviourists'. This text would be particularly interesting to any student intending to study psychology beyond A-level. Hunt gives an extremely thorough and comprehensive account of the history of psychology.

8

Study aids

IMPROVING YOUR ESSAY WRITING SKILLS

At this point in the book you will have acquired the knowledge necessary to tackle the exam itself. Answering exam questions is a skill which this chapter shows you how to improve. Examiners obviously have first-hand knowledge about what goes wrong in exams. For example, candidates frequently do not answer the question which has been set; rather they answer the one that they hoped would come up, or they do not make effective use of the knowledge they have but just 'dump their psychology' on the page and hope the examiner will sort it out for them. A grade 'C' answer usually contains appropriate material but tends to be limited in detail and commentary. To lift such an answer to a grade 'A' or 'B' may require no more than a little more detail, better use of material and coherent organisation. It is important to appreciate that it may not involve writing at any greater length, but might even necessitate the elimination of passages which do not add to the quality of the answer and some elaboration of those which do.

By studying the essays presented in this chapter and the examiner's comments, you can learn how to turn your grade 'C' answer into a grade 'A'. Typically it only involves an extra 4 marks out of 24. Please note that marks given by the examiner in the practice essays should be used as a guide only and are not definitive. They represent the 'raw' marks which would be likely to be given to answers to AQA (A) questions.

In the AQA (A) examination, an examiner would award a maximum of 12 marks for knowledge and understanding (called Assessment Objective 1 – AO1) and 12 marks for evaluation, analysis and commentary (Assessment Objective 2 – AO2). The details of this marking scheme are given in Appendix C of Paul Humphreys' title in this series, *Exam Success in AEB Psychology*, and the forthcoming title *Exam Success in AQA(A) Psychology*. Remember that these are the raw marks and not the same as those given on the examination certificate received ultimately by the candidate because all examining boards are required to use a common standardised system called the Uniform Mark Scale (UMS), which adjusts all raw scores to a single standard across all boards.

The essays given here are notionally written by an 18-year-old in 30 minutes and marked bearing that in mind. It is important when writing to such a tight time limit that you make every sentence count. Each essay in this chapter is followed by detailed comments about its strengths and weaknesses. The most common problems to watch out for are:

- Failure to answer the question but reproducing a model answer to a similar question which you have pre-learned.
- Not delivering the right balance between description and evaluation/analysis. Remember they are always weighted 50/50.
- Writing 'everything you know' about a topic in the hope that something will get credit and the examiner will sort your work out for you. Remember that excellence demands selectivity, so improvements can often be made by removing material which is irrelevant to the question set and elaborating material which is relevant.
- Failing to use your material effectively. It is not enough to place the information on the page but you must also show the examiner that you are using it to make a particular point.

For more ideas on how to write good essays you should consult *Exam Success in AEB Psychology* and the forthcoming title *Exam Success in AQA(A) Psychology* (by Paul Humphreys) in this series.

Practice essay

Discuss the free will versus determinism debate as it applies to two theoretical orientations in psychology.

*Starting point: This is a 24-mark question. It is very important to note that the debate concerning free will and determinsim should be discussed with **two** theoretical orientations or approaches in mind. Candidates who attempt this question should first ask themselves whether or not they have a clear idea of which **two** orientations they are going to discuss. Candidates discussing only one will receive only partial marks. Examiners refer to this type of answer as 'partial performance'. On the other hand, candidates discussing **more** than two will only receive credit for the best two that they present. Discussing more than two orientations is likely to result in a waste of valuable time in the examination. However, it is permissible and can be helpful to **mention** a third or even a fourth orientation/approach. But this should only be done if it serves to comment upon, or in some way add to, the two main approaches that you have chosen to discuss.*

*Finally, remember that this question asks you to **discuss** two orientations. Knowledge and understanding, **AO1**, of the two approaches that you choose can be credited with a maximum of 12 marks by the examiner. In order to obtain marks for **AO2**, your answer would need to demonstrate an ability to evaluate and comment upon the orientations. It might also involve showing that you have a broad range of knowledge of issues related to psychology generally.*

AQA (AEB) 1998

Candidate's answer

The following answer has been written by the author. It has not been provided or approved by the AQA and it may not necessarily constitute the only answer.

In this essay I will discuss the free will versus determinism debate as it applies to the following two orientations in psychology: (1) behaviourism and (2) the biological approach to psychology.

Behaviourists, such as Skinner, did not believe in free will at all. This was because, in his experiments with rats and pigeons, he found that he was able to 'shape' an animal's behaviour with rewards and punishments. He believed from these observations that, because he was controlling the environment of the animal and was actually able to control what the animal did, then how could the animal be said to be behaving freely? For Skinner, all behaviour is determined by the environment. In fact, another behaviourist, Watson, claimed that he could turn any child into any type of person, for example, a doctor, a lawyer, or even a thief, if he was able to have complete control over the child's environment.

In terms of the nature–nurture debate, behaviourism very strongly pushes the nurture side of the argument. For both Skinner and Watson, free will did not really exist. It was an illusion. People think that they are free, but, just like Skinner's rats and pigeons, their behaviour is actually the result of reward and punishment. In other words, a direct result of the environment into which they are placed.

Another experimenter, Pavlov, found that he could make a dog salivate to the sound of a bell. He could do this if he presented the dog with food and the sound of a bell at the same time. Dogs salivate when presented with food, but do not normally do so at the sound of a bell. But Pavlov's dogs learned to associate the bell with the food and eventually would salivate when just the bell was sounded. Again, the animal's behaviour, salivating at the sound of a bell, is determined, or controlled, by the environment. It is not free because the animal does not choose to salivate at the sound of the bell. Quite the opposite is the case: it is the experimenter who controls what the animal does.

One of the main problems with behaviourism's approach/orientation to psychology is that it is difficult to prove that what Skinner and Pavlov found to happen with animals can be applied to human beings.

Biological orientation will now be examined. This approach concentrates on the idea that all of our behaviour is a result of what goes on at the biological level. This is also known as a form of reductionism, because all behaviour can be said to be reduced to the biological level. For example, the biological approach would push the idea that we get angry, hungry, emotional, thirsty, etc. because of what is happening within our bodies, and particularly within the brain. People who have had a stroke, for example, might be unable to speak because the stroke has damaged the areas of the brain responsible for producing language. A psychologist, Norman Geschwind, also found that people with strokes that affected the areas of the brain responsible for emotions will often not display appropriate emotions. Experiments on rats have shown that stimulating a particular part of the hypothalamus will make the rat drink much too much water. So the above examples clearly show that biological events determine behaviour in all animals (including humans, of course, because human beings are animals). If this is the case, how can behaviour be said to be the result of free will?

Hormones can also influence behaviour. This is another example of biological events determining how people behave.

Examiner's comments

This candidate has written an appropriate and sensible answer which does address the question set. The essay starts with a clear indication of which two orientations are to be discussed, and the two are actually then presented here. The second paragraph is factually quite correct. It is quite true that behaviourists hold this strong stance against free will. Watson's famous claim is usefully highlighted. The third paragraph here demonstrates evidence of a breadth of knowledge (AO2) because the candidate quite correctly identifies the fact that behaviourism vehemently comes down on the side of nurture (environment) in the nature–nurture debate. This is an example of the way in which other issues/debates can be brought into an essay without 'taking over'. In other words, the candidate has not gone on to waste a lot of time writing about the nature–nurture debate. (This is the kind of thing that some candidates tend to do when they have prepared for a question solely relating to the nature–nurture debate. That is they sometimes tend to try to make what they have prepared 'fit' the actual question set.) A breadth of knowledge is also displayed where the candidate correctly refers to the issue of *reductionism* at the start of the section which covers the biological approach to psychology.

The balance in terms of the amount of time spent writing about each of the two orientations is about right. In terms of AO1, which examines the student's knowledge and understanding, this answer would probably score about 8 out of 12. Content is appropriate and correct but could have been explained a little more clearly. The material presented concerning the biological approach is 'thrown in', so to speak, rather than 'talked through' in a logical and connected manner. The essay ends in a rather abrupt manner. The influence of hormones is correctly included here, but an illustrative example would have convinced the examiner that the candidate *really* understood just how hormonal activity can determine behaviour. (For instance, the example provided below in ***research article 3*** might have worked well.)

In terms of critical evaluation – the *'discuss'* part of this question – this essay would probably earn about 5 marks out of 12. The fifth paragraph makes a correct criticism, but the candidate misses the opportunity to indicate just *why* behaviourism actually is a theoretical approach/orientation to psychology. For example, it is true that comparisons of rats and pigeons to human beings are problematic, but behaviourists insisted that, despite such difficulties, it was *theoretically* feasible that human behaviour (although much more complex) could logically be explained in terms of the basic 'building blocks' of associative learning. A breadth of knowledge could have been demonstrated if the candidate had, for example, written about the ways in which the principles of behaviourism have indeed been applied to human behaviour. In clinical psychology, for example, so-called token economies have claimed success in treating some less severe disorders such as depression. Critical discussion of behaviourism could have included, for example, some comment as to the impracticality of actually testing Watson's claim.

So, this essay would probably have earned a total of about 13 marks out of 24. This would be likely to be the equivalent of a grade C at A-level. The examiner's comments above should clearly indicate just how the candidate could 'push up' the essay so that it might earn a grade A.

KEY RESEARCH SUMMARIES

Article 1

Blakemore, C. and Cooper, G. F. (1970) Development of the Brain depends on the Visual Environment, *Nature*, 228: 477–478.

Introduction

Individual neurones in the visual cortex of the cat are known to be particularly 'tuned into', or sensitive to, lines and edges at particular orientations in the visual field. Research conducted prior to the present investigation includes Hirch and Spinelli (1970). Here kittens were reared in an environment whereby one eye was exposed only to viewing vertical stripes, the other eye to horizontal stripes. From studying 25 neurones in the visual cortex, it was found that all were monocularly 'tuned'. That is to say that they appeared to be 'tuned into' responding only to visual in-puts from one eye. It was also found that in all but one case, the orientation to which the particular neurones seemed 'responsive' was either vertical or horizontal, and that this corresponded with the orientation of the visual stimuli to which that eye had been exposed. This provides clear evidence for the way in which the visual system is 'shaped' by the environment to which it is exposed.

Method

The present research also involved kittens. But here the kittens were exposed to visual stimuli using normal binocular vision. After being reared for the first two weeks of life in darkness, the kittens were placed in a specially designed visual 'world' for 5 hours per day until the age of 5 months. This was a 'world' which was specially designed to allow them visual in-put of sharply contrasting black-and-white stripes in either vertical or horizontal orientation. Special black collars prevented the kittens from viewing their own bodies. This was to ensure that their only visual in-put consisted of either vertical or horizontal stimuli.

Results

Some of the effects of these specially designed visual environments seemed to the researchers to be quite permanent and to be common to all of the kittens. They would often bump into things, such as table legs, and would try to touch objects in their visual field but which were actually far out of their reach. The differences between the two experimental groups, however, were of much more interest. The behaviour of the kittens was carefully studied. Each group of kittens seemed quite blind to visual stimuli presented at the orientation to which the *other* group of kittens had been exposed. An advancing sheet of perspex would only provoke a startled response if it had lines which matched the orientation to which they had become tuned. Having examined the kittens' behaviour, the researchers then anaesthetised the kittens in order to study individual neurones within the visual cortex. Here it was found that not one of the neurones in one group of kittens showed a preference or sensitivity to stimuli presented at an orientation corresponding to the stimuli to which the other group had been exposed, and only 12 neurones seemed responsive to a stimulus within 45 degrees of the 'opposite' orientation. Statistical analysis, employing the chi squared test, revealed that the chance of these results occurring purely by chance was 1 in 100,000 ($p < 0.00001$).

Discussion

Blakemore and Cooper conclude that it would seem that the visual cortex has a certain 'plasticity' about it. Neurones, so it would appear, tune into the visual world to which they are exposed. Undoubtedly, neurones even change their natural orientation in order to adapt to the type of visual stimulus that tends to present itself, thus adaptively reflecting the probability of occurrence of particular features of their visual world.

Article 2

Sperry, R. (1984) Consciousness, Personal Identity and the Divided Brain, *Neuropsychologica*, 22, 661–673.

This is an important and well-known article that critically reviews a large amount of research into the mental capacities of the right and left halves of the brain following surgical separation of the two hemispheres. This type of surgery, known as commissurotomy, has been performed in rare cases in order to control severe epilepsy. This article provokes serious questions concerning the mind–body problem because, post-surgery, each half of the brain seems to 'live' an independent existence. These studies of 'split-brain' patients would seem to provoke the following question: as both hemispheres seem to retain a rich mental life, albeit with differing abilities, where does the person who has undergone such surgery now 'reside'? If, as the materialist position concerning the mind–body problems would have it, the 'mind' equals brain processes, then does a split-brain also equal two very separate minds?

Following surgical separation, the split-brain patient has two disconnected hemispheres which both would appear to function at a high level. However, most conscious mental life experienced by one hemisphere does not appear to be communicated to the other, and vice versa. The left hemisphere, for example, sees visual stimuli in the right half of the visual field, while stimuli to the left of the field are experienced by the right half of the brain. Sperry points out that, following such surgical intervention, cerebral representations of the limbs are also 'divided'. Thus, such patients would typically report that an object felt with the right hand is perceived mainly by the 'person' inhabiting the left hemisphere.

Intuitively many commentators had previously argued that the 'real' person living within a split-brain really must reside in the left hemisphere, where language is largely located, with the right hemisphere carrying on in a zombie-like state. Sperry, however, regards this as an attitude which clings to the idea that what separates humans from other animals is our language abilities. He refers, therefore, to some of his own previous research (Sperry, 1961) with cats and infra-human primates which seems to provide clear evidence that *both* hemispheres could post-surgically remember, learn and perceive equally competently.

Sperry clearly regards the left hemisphere as being somewhat 'privileged' because, being the half of the brain largely responsible for language, it can 'speak its mind'. Just because the right hemisphere has little or no 'voice', this does not imply that it has an impoverished mental life. To add weight to this argument, this article cites evidence that the right hemisphere is clearly able to make cognitive decisions, to reason non-verbally, and to carry out inventive solutions to problems. An indication that the right hemisphere does have consciousness includes the fact that it generates normal facial expressions expressing satisfaction when it (the right hemisphere) successfully completes a task. And indeed annoyance with 'its self' when it makes errors.

Sperry also cites demonstrations which clearly illustrate that the right hemisphere possesses an 'emotional side'. Appropriate reactions were observed to pictures presented to the right hemisphere of highly affect-laden items such as photographs of family, pets, and personal belongings.

As with many areas of psychology, studies of 'split-brain' patients have wider applications to the 'real world'. Sperry insists here that our education system has an over-emphasis upon those abilities typically the domain of the left hemisphere. Schools tend to focus strongly on the so-called 'three R's' (Reading, Writing, and Arithmetic). This Sperry clearly regards as a discrimination 'against the non-verbal, non-mathematical half of the brain which has its own perceptual-mechanical-spatial mode of apprehension and reasoning' (p. 667).

Article 3

Reinisch, J. M. (1981) Prenatal Exposure to Synthetic Progestins Increases Potential for Aggression in Humans, *Science*, 211: 1171–1173.

Introduction

This research article relates clearly to three of the major debates covered in this book.

1 In terms of the nature–nurture debate, this research serves as an illustration of the fact that the effects of the environment – nurture – must include the conditions to which an individual is exposed *in utero*, not just from birth onwards.
2 If hormones can be seen to drive behaviour, this clearly can be seen to relate to the free will/determinism debate. What might appear to be 'choice' might actually be, at least to some degree, hormonally driven/determined.
3 This article provides evidence for reductionism because it suggests that aggressive behaviour might have its origin at the hormonal level. In other words, that aggression is the 'expression' of hormonal influence.

The hormone progesterone essentially ensures that the menstrual cycle in the pregnant woman ceases. This secures the pregnancy and prevents, for example, the breakdown of the lining of the womb. The authors begin this article by pointing out that between 1950 and 1980 millions of pregnant women had been treated with synthetic estrogen and progesterone in order to avoid miscarriage or to treat other pregnancy-related problems. Other research indicates that synthetic progesterone administered orally to pregnant women can have masculinising effects on the developing child. Such effects can include the development of male-like features in the genitalia in as many as 18 per cent of human female offspring exposed in the womb to this synthetic hormone. A study, described in Chapter Two, by Meyer-Bahlburg et al. (1995) indicates that it also would appear to play a role in the offspring's sexual preference as an adult. The present study examines possible effects of *in utero* exposure to synthetic progesterone on levels of aggression.

Method

Seventeen females and eight males, whose mothers had been treated with synthetic progesterone, were asked to indicate which kind of behaviour they thought they were most likely to engage in when confronted with a variety of conflict situations. After each of a series of six situations was described, the participants were asked to choose which type of response they thought they would be most likely to make. The choices were:

  (i)   physical aggression
 (ii)   verbal aggression
(iii)   withdrawal from the situation
(iv)   non-aggressive coping with the other/s involved in the situation

Were a participant to select, for example, physical aggression for each of the six situations described, then a maximum score for aggression would be obtained. Each participant's score was then compared with the score obtained from a sibling of the same sex who had not been exposed to synthetic progesterone. This comparison with siblings was an attempt to match genetic and environmental variables.

Results

Exposure to synthetic progesterone would appear to have an effect upon levels of aggression. The exposed females chose physical aggression significantly more often than did their non-exposed sisters. Similarly, a higher score for aggression was found in the group of exposed males when compared with their brothers. No significant difference was found for either males or females, however, in the number of times verbal aggression was chosen. It was expected that a comparison of unexposed males with unexposed females would show that males were more likely to respond aggressively. This was found to be the case.

Glossary

The first occurrence of each of these terms is highlighted in **bold** type in the main text.

associative learning   In operant conditioning this describes how an animal learns to associate its behaviour with whatever outcome it produces. Classical conditioning concerns the learned association, or 'pairing', of a stimulus that produces a reflex response with a neutral stimulus, which does not produce the reflex response. After such pairing, the neutral stimulus alone can produce the reflex response because associative learning has taken place.

behavioural ecology   The study of how an animal's behaviour is shaped by the evolutionary pressures arising from its ecological circumstances, including its social environment.

category error   The confusion inherent in mistakenly believing something to belong to a particular group or class. For example, if the 'mind' is not a physical 'thing' then, unlike the rest of the body, it cannot become 'ill'. Thus the very idea of 'mental illness' is the mistaken outcome of a category error.

counter-balancing   An experimental procedure employed to eliminate possible order effects. If participants are to be compared on their performance across two tasks, then half of them would do task *x* first and half would do task *y* first. Thus any order effects, such as fatigue or practice, would be 'spread' equally across the two tasks.

diathesis-stress   An approach to the cause of psychiatric disorders which assumes a biological predisposition, *diathesis*, and an environmental source of *stress* that precipitates or triggers a particular disorder.

dizygotic   Dizygotic twins result from the (almost) simultaneous fertilisation of two eggs by two sperm cells. Hence, such twins are no more similar genetically than any other two siblings born separately.

EEG   Abbreviation for electroencephalogram: a record of the changes in electrical potential of the brain. This is a non-intrusive procedure achieved by attaching electrodes to the scalp.

epistemology   Theory of the methods used to gain knowledge about the world and the analysis of the status, or 'truth value', of the knowledge obtained by particular methods.

ethnomethodology   An approach in psychology and sociology for gaining knowledge about socially negotiated, created, 'realities'. The emphasis is on gaining access to and making explicit the rules that underlie – and are *understood* by particular social group members themselves to underlie – such negotiation.

external validity   The extent to which the results of investigations within the laboratory can be 'mapped onto' the real world outside.

extinction   The eventual disappearance of a learned response in the absence of whatever was reinforcing the response, in the case of operant conditioning, or in the discontinued pairing of the conditioned stimulus with the unconditioned stimulus, in the case of classical conditioning.

idiographic   Related to that which is unique or individualistic about people.

individual differences   An area of psychology that concerns itself with psychological characteristics or dimensions along which individuals can be shown to differ, such as personality or intelligence.

infra-human   In terms of evolutionary development, lower, or inferior, to human beings.

intentionality   Mental states have 'intentionality', meaning that they are *about* something in the outer world of events, objects, etc.

internal validity   The degree to which an experimenter is sure about the relationship between dependent and independent variables. The degree to which s/he is confident in causal links *within* an experimental set-up.

introspection   The act of looking into, and reporting on, one's own mental events and processes.

law of parsimony   The belief that if two theories seem equally valid, then the less complicated one should be adopted.

learned helplessness   A condition generated by continuously exposing an animal to unpleasant conditions, such as electric shocks, from which there is no escape. When eventually an escape route is provided, the animal, having learned that all previous behaviour had failed to effect escape, will refuse to do anything. The animal has learned from the results of its previous behaviour that it cannot help itself.

mental way-stations   The idea that there is some mental activity that occurs between a stimulus and an animal's response, or between an animal's response and the effects of that response.

monozygotic   Monozygotic twins are genetically identical because they are the result of the fertilisation of one egg.

nomothetic   Related to similarities between individuals. Concerned with that which is general or universal among people.

paradigm   The set of attitudes, values and established methodological procedures which are generally agreed upon by members of a particular discipline, for example, psychology.

phylogenetic   Relating to the evolution and development of a particular species, as opposed to 'ontogenetic' which refers to the development of a particular member of a species.

randomisation   Similar procedure to **counter-balancing**, except that participants are allocated quite at random to which of the two tasks they are to do first.

refractive index   The extent to which light is 'bent', or refracted, as it passes from one medium to another is a constant and thus can be calculated in advance using the established index for those two particular media – for example, air and water.

replicable   An experiment is replicable if another researcher can repeat it at a later point in time using exactly the same procedure as adopted by the original researcher.

sampling error   A term used to describe any difference that exists between the true value of a measure of a population and the value obtained from the sample of that population actually measured.

slips of the tongue   Often referred to as 'Freudian slips', these refer to 'errors' in speech which reveal an individual's subconscious desires.

spontaneous recovery   The reappearance of a learned response that had undergone **extinction**.

standard deviation   A measure of variability of a sample of scores from the mean of that sample.

token economy   A form of behaviour therapy whereby the patient is rewarded with tokens for exhibiting particular desired or 'target' behaviour. These tokens being exchangeable for rewards that the patient values, such as cigarettes or chocolate.

References

Baker, R. (1999) A bit of who's your father? *The Times Higher Education Supplement*, p. 17, 29 January 1999.

Bannister, D. (1968) The myth of physiological psychology. *Bulletin of the British Psychological Society*, 21, 229–231.

Becker, J. (1977) *Hitler's Children: The Story of the Baader-Meinhof Gang*. London: Michael Joseph.

Blakemore, C. and Cooper, G. F. (1970) Development of the brain depends on the visual environment. *Nature*, 228, 477–478.

Brown, R. (1986) *Social Psychology*, 2nd edn. New York: Free Press.

Cochrane, R. (1983) *The Social Creation of Mental Illness*. London: Longman.

Ebbesen, E. B. and Konečni, V. J. (1975) Decision making and information integration in the courts: the setting of bail. *Journal of Personality and Social Psychology*, 32, 805–821.

Ellis, W. D. (1938) *A Source Book of Gestalt Psychology*. London: Routledge & Kegan Paul.

Ferris, P. (1998) *Dr. Freud: A Life*. London: Pimlico.

Gale, A. (1979) Psychophysiology: a bridge between disciplines. Inaugural Lecture, University of Southampton.

Goswami, U. (2000) How babies think. *The Times Higher Education Supplement*, p. 28, 5 May 2000.

Gould, J. L. and Gould, C. G. (1998) Reasoning in animals. *Scientific American*, 9, 52–59.

Gregory, R. J. (1996) *Psychological Testing: History, Principles & Applications*. Boston: Allyn & Bacon.

Gregory, R. L. (1966) *Eye and Brain*. London: Weidenfeld & Nicolson.

Gregory, R. L. (1970) *The Intelligent Eye*. London: Weidenfeld & Nicolson.

Harré, R. and Secord, P. F. (1972) *The Explanation of Social Behaviour*. Oxford: Basil Blackwell.

Helson, H. (1933) The fundamental propositions of gestalt psychology. *Psychology Review*, 40, 13–32.

Horswill, M. S. and McKenna, F. P. (1997) Measuring, manipulating and understanding drivers' speed choice. *Behavioural Research in Road Safety*, vol. VII. Transport Laboratory, Crowthorne, Berks.

Hospers, J. (1990) *An Introduction to Philosophical Analysis*, 3rd edn. London: Routledge.

Hubel, D. H. and Wiesel, T. N. (1959) Receptive fields of single neurons in the cat's striate cortex. *Journal of Physiology*, 148, 574–591.

Jung, C. G. (1989) Foreword in R. Wilhelm and C. F. Baynes (trans.) *I Ching: or Book of Changes*. London: Penguin.

Kaplan, R. M. and Saccuzzo, D. P. (1999) *Psychological Testing: Principles, Applications & Issues*. Boston: Brooks-Cole Publishing Company.

Köhler, W. (1925) *The Mentality of Apes*. New York: Harcourt Brace Jovanovich.

Laing, R. D. (1959) *The Divided Self*. London: Penguin [1990].

Laing, R. D. (1967) *The Politics of Experience and The Bird of Paradise*. London: Penguin [1990].

Laing, R. D. and Esterson, A. (1970 edition) *Sanity, Madness and the Family*. London: Penguin [1990].

Lawrence, M. (1999) Driving behaviour, unpublished dissertation, The Manchester Metropolitan University.

Lichtenstein, P. (2000) *The Daily Telegraph*, p. 13, 14 July 2000.

Lorenz, K. Z. (1966) *On Aggression*. London: Methuen.

Meyer-Bahlburg, H. F. L., Ehrhardt, A. A., Rosen, L. R. and Gruen, R. S. (1995) Prenatal estrogens and the development of homosexual orientation. *Developmental Psychology*, 31 (1), 12–21.

Milgram, S. (1963) Behavioural study of obedience. *Journal of Abnormal and Social Psychology*, 67, 371–378.

Miller, G. A. (1956) The magical number seven, plus or minus two: some limits on our capacity for processing information. *Psychology Review*, 63, 81–97.

Miller, J. (ed.) (1983) *States of Mind*. London: British Broadcasting Corporation.

O'Connor, D. J. (1971) *Free Will*. New York: Doubleday.

Pavlov, I. (1960) *Conditioned Reflexes: An Investigation into the Physiological Activity of the Cerebral Cortex*. New York: Dover [1927].

Penfield, W. and Rasmussen, T. (1950) *The Cerebral Cortex of Man: A Clinical Study of Localisation*. Boston: Little Brown.

Reinisch, J. M. (1981) Prenatal exposure to synthetic progestins increases potential for aggression in humans. *Science*, 211, 1171–1173

Ridley, M. (1994) *The Red Queen*. London: Penguin.

Rose, S. (1976) *The Conscious Brain*. Harmondsworth: Penguin.

Rosenfield, D. (2000) *The Times Higher Education Supplement*, p. 2, 15 October 2000.

Russell, J. G. B. (1982) The rationale for primitive delivery positions. *British Journal of Obstetrics and Gynaecology*, 89, 712–715.

Ryave, A. L. and Schenkein, J. N. (1974) Notes on the art of walking, in R. Turner (ed.) *Ethomethodology*. Harmondsworth: Penguin.

Sartre, J.-P. (1943) *Being and Nothingness*. London: Routledge [1993].

Sartre, J.-P. (1946) *Existentialism and Humanism*. London: Methuen [1948].

Sartre, J.-P. (1965) *Nausea*. London: Penguin.

Searle, J. (1991) *Minds, Brains & Science*. London: Penguin.

Shields, J. (1978) Genetics, in J. K. Wing (ed.) *Schizophrenia: Towards a New Synthesis*. London: Academic Press.

Skinner, B. F. (1938) *The Behaviour of Organisms*. New York: Appleton-Century-Crofts.

Skinner, B. F. (1960) Pigeons in a pelican. *American Psychologist*, 15, 28–37.

Soares, C. (1984) Left-hemisphere language lateralization in bilinguals: use of the concurrent activities paradigm. *Brain and Language*, 23, 86–96.

Sperry, R. (1961) Cerebral organization and behaviour. *Science*, 133, 1749–1757.

Sperry, R. (1984) Consciousness, personal identity and the divided brain. *Neuropsychologica*, 22, 661–673.

Stoner, J. A. F. (1961) A comparison of individual and group decisions including risk, unpublished thesis, Massachusetts Institute of Technology, School of Management.

Thorndike, E. L. (1911) *Animal Intelligence*. New York: Macmillan.

Tinbergen, N. (1951) *The Study of Instinct*. Oxford: Oxford University Press.

Wann, T. W. (ed.) (1964) *Behaviourism and Phenomenology*. Chicago: University of Chicago Press.

Warden, C. J. (ed.) (1931) *Animal Motivation: Experimental Studies on the Albino Rat*. New York: Columbia University Press.

Warnock, M. (1992) *Existentialism*. Oxford: Oxford University Press [1970].

Watson, J. B. (1924) *Behaviourism*. Chicago: University of Chicago Press.

Weiskrantz, L. (1986) *Blindsight: A Case Study and Implications*. Oxford: Clarendon Press.

Wertheimer, M. (1923) *Investigations of the Doctrine of Gestalt* (English trans. by W. D. Ellis, 1938). London: Routledge & Kegan-Paul.

Zajonc, R. B. (1965) Social facilitation. *Science*, 149, 269–274.

Index